Let there be Melomels!

Fruit Meads designed to inspire your Imagination

By: Robert Ratliff

Edited by Vicky Rowe Gotmead.com/Craft Beverage Marketing

DEDICATION

To my sons Blake and Derek. I continue to push and stretch my boundaries to impress on them by example that the only true limitations you face in life are those you choose to place on yourself.

THIS PAGE INTENTIONALLY LEFT BLANK

TABLE OF CONTENTS

DEDICATION..III

PREFACE..8

AUTHOR'S NOTE..10

FORWARD 11

INTRODUCTION...13

TYPES OF FRUIT 14

YEAST (Brands, Strains, & Characteristics) 20

SWEETNESS LEVELS 22

CALCULATING ABV (Specific Gravity & Brix) 23

NUTRIENTS (Types and their use).............................24

TAILORED ORGANIC STAGGERED NUTRIENT ADDITIONS 25

NUTRIENT ADDITION SCHEDULE...........................26

BJCP CATEGORIES (Beer Judge Certification Program)...................27

EQUIPMENT LIST 28

READING A HYDROMETER..29

UNIT CONVERSIONS (US to Metric).........................31

CALCULATIONS & FORMULAS...................................32

RECIPES 33

M2A – Cysers (Apple Meads)......................................35
    Oaked Orange Blossom Cyser....................................36
    Simple "Dry" Cyser 38
    Simple "Semi-Sweet" Cyser..40
    Simple "Sweet" Cyser 42
    Simple "Dessert/Sack" Cyser 44

M2B – Pyments (Grape Meads) 46
    Concord Pyment "Semi-Sweet" Grape Mead.............47
    Muscadine Pyment "Semi-Sweet" Grape Mead.........49
    White Pyment "Semi-Sweet" Grape Mead..................51

M2C – Berry Meads..**53**
   Black Currant (Black Mead) 54
   Blackberry Blast "Sweet" Melomel................................56
   Blueberry Bliss "Semi-Sweet" Melomel.......................58
   Cranberry "Semi-Sweet" Mead....................................60
   Raspberry "Sweet" Melomel...62
   Strawberry "Semi-Sweet" Melomel..............................64

M2D – Stone Fruit Meads...**66**
   Cherry Melomel (Sour)..67
   Mango Melomel "Semi-Sweet" 69

M2E – Other/Mixed Fruit Meads..**71**
   Apple-Blackberry "Sweet" Cyser..................................72
   Apple-Blueberry-Cranberry "Semi-Sweet" Cyser.......74
   Apple-Blueberry "Semi-Sweet" Cyser.........................76
   Apple-Cranberry "Sweet" Cyser 78
   Apple-Raspberry "Sweet" Cyser 80
   Apple-Sour Cherry "Semi-Sweet" Cyser......................82
   Black Currant-Blueberry-Blackberry 84
   Blackberry-Blueberry-Raspberry-Sour Cherry Mead....86
   Blackberry-Blueberry "Semi-Sweet" Mead..................88
   Blueberry - Black Currant Mead 90
   Blueberry-Blackberry-Raspberry-Sour Cherry Mead....92
   Blueberry-Blackberry-Raspberry-Strawberry-Sour Cherry....94
   Blueberry-Blackberry-Raspberry-Strawberry "Semi-Sweet" 96
   Coconut Melomel 98
   Cranberry-Raspberry "Semi-Sweet" Mead................100
   Elderberry-Blackberry "Sack" Mead..........................102
   Orange - Mango "Semi-Sweet" Mead 104
   Orange-Pineapple-Coconut (Escape to the Tropics)....106
   Orange - Pineapple Melomel 108
   Orange – Raspberry "Semi-Sweet" Melomel 110
   Pineapple – Sour Cherry "Sweet" Mead.....................112
   Pineapple Melomel "Semi-Sweet" 114
   Pineapple-Mango Melomel "Semi-Sweet" 116
   Strawberry - Kiwi "Semi-Sweet" Melomel..................118

M4B – Historical Meads (Polish Melomels) **120**
  TYPES & DESCRIPTIONS 120
  DEVELOPING YOUR PRIMARY 124
  CONTROLLING ACIDITY (pH) 126

YEAST REHYDRATION 127
POLISH MEAD RECIPES 129
  Trójniak 26 130
  Trójniak 41 132
  Trójniak 43 134
  Trójniak 54 137
  Trójniak 64 139
  Trójniak 83 142
  Trójniak 102 144
  Trójniak 103 "Sofia" 146
  Trójniak 104 148
  Trójniak 108 150
  Trójniak 109 152
  Trójniak 114 154
  Trójniak 117 156
  Trójniak 121 158
  Trójniak 134 160
AN ALTERNATIVE METHOD 162
  Trójniak Agrestniak 163
  Trójniak Smorodyniak 165
  Trójniak Wiśniak z Czeremchą 167
  Trójniak Wiśniak 169
DWOJNIAK PREPARATION 171
ENHANCING YOUR YEAST STARTER 172
  Dwójniak Aroniak 173

GLOSSARY OF TERMS 176

BIBLIOGRAPHY 178
  WEBSITES: 178
  BOOKS: 178

INDEX 179

ABOUT THE AUTHOR: 183

PREFACE

As with most aspiring authors (or Mead Makers), there is always that person or persons who inspire us to reach out and do what we do. In my case this honor lies with my wife and two sons. They've always been supportive of my hobbies and without their continued encouragement I would most certainly be less than I am today. With that in mind, I'd like to dedicate this book to Janette for her years of patience with me, to Blake for showing me how to tackle new things without fearing the unknown, and to Derek for motivating me to follow my interests no matter where they might lead. You three make me want to keep stretching out of that comfort zone to see what I can achieve in life.

With the release of this second book in the series, I thought it appropriate to take a moment and explain how this latest endeavor came to be.

I was finishing up the final details on my first effort _The Big Book of Mead Recipes_ when my son asked me what I was going to write next. I mentioned that I might consider writing a sequel since I had so much fun on the first one. He thought that would be pretty cool, but then, being the sharp individual he is, suggested that I do an entire series of books with each being based on a certain type or category of mead. I thought about this for a few minutes and decided that it was actually a great idea. Some people while interested in making Melomels might not be interested in Metheglins or Braggots at all. Why should those people have to buy an across the board type of book when they could get one filled solely with recipes they might actually want to make? With that realization, a project was born.

In this series, we will undertake a journey through several types/styles of mead and I will strive in each to provide you with a varied selection of recipes to choose from to whet the imagination and to get those creative juices flowing. As I've noted in the past, I'm not promising you award winning meads, but I've made a few and my style is pretty consistent.

Once again, I'll be dealing with primarily 1-gallon batch yields in these recipes. They're easy to put together without breaking the bank and let's face it, how many of us can afford to take a chance on a 5-gallon (or larger) batch that we may not like in the end?

The one caveat to this standard policy lies within the new Polish Recipe section. That selection of recipes will be presented in the way that I receive them. This is in order to preserve their authenticity and to properly present them as they were intended. If you read my first book and have gone though this one, you've learned enough to be able to scale them down if that's your real goal.

With that in mind, I hope you enjoy the book and I hope it takes your interest in making good Melomels to a new level either through my recipes or by the ideas is inspires you to try on your own. Free your minds and ideas will follow.

Cheers!

Rob

AUTHOR'S NOTE

Before you begin delving into the recipes I've provided in the following pages, I'll once again leave you with these three important details before you start your preparations.

First: The volume of honey I'm dictating to be used in each recipe is based on a calculation that states that honey will provide 35 fermentation points (0.035) per pound of honey. This is not a carved in stone number. Different honeys will have a different percentage of sugar content. This baseline is an average percentage based on several varying types of honey and is generally agreed on as the standard. I've found this to be the case with several online calculators as well. In my own formulae, I've modified a few factors to assist in generating recipes based on desired results. Instead of figuring honey first and gravities later, I've adjusted the calculations to allow the brewer to decide sweetness and percentage of alcohol content first and then the result to be how much honey that will take. They additionally add the sugar content of any fruit additions you might want to add based on the weight and sugar content of the fruit.

Second: Regarding the Cyser recipes or any recipe using apple juice as a foundation. The base gravity reading for the apple juice was taken using MARTINELLI's Apple Juice. Different brands or apple types may vary this input.

Third: I've given approximate fermentation points per pound of fruit in the fruit descriptions. These are approximate values based on sugar content/lb. There is most definitely a margin of error to factor in, but the numbers here should get you close enough to your target for ballpark estimates.

These calculations are currently being looked at with the possibility of converting them to a handy App for a mobile device. They will eventually take into account both meads and cysers.

Please adjust all starting gravities accordingly in order to achieve the desired results. This can be done either by adding more liquid or more honey depending on which way your starting gravity needs to be moved.

FORWARD

There are a lot of mead books out there, and more being written all the time. Many of these books are focused on making mead, providing in-depth advice on processes and techniques, and offering recipes to represent the techniques. But until now, there haven't really been any dedicated recipe collections.

Well there are now.

When Rob released his first book *The Big Book of Mead Recipes*, he gave us a new way to look at mead recipe books. Instead of offering us another book on mead basics or a lot of mead chemistry, Rob offered us a book chock full of recipes that intermediate and expert mead makers alike could sink their teeth into. A book that inspired the imagination and made the reader ponder that age-old question "I wonder what would happen if I added this?"

With the release of this second book in his "Let There Be Mead!" series, Rob shows that he's not just a one-hit wonder. He's now taking on several popular mead categories one at a time to give you some real insight into each. His main goal as always is to show the way to making better meads and to inspire more people to try and develop their own unique style and approach as their skill levels in the craft grow.

As I mentioned in the first book, and it's worth repeating here, Rob is what I term a "Natural Meadmaker". He seems to be able to instinctively design meads that taste great, and is a dab hand at managing his fermentations.

It's not just that Rob is an instinctive mead maker either. He also, and more importantly, recognizes that one can learn whatever one needs to, if one is willing to seek out information and industry leaders and to ask questions. Making great meads means always being willing to learn and adapt to new ideas and concepts in brewing and fermentation.

Rob is dedicated to making awesome mead. His obsession with the craft means that he is always open to learning different brewing styles, how to balance new recipes, how to improve his methods for recipe development, and continuing to learn improved batch management techniques. Incorporating the best from each new process or idea he learns into his own method, Rob's meads and his brewing habits have changed and evolved along with the industry.

Enjoy your mead making, and let us know what you think! Email me at gotmead@gotmead.com , and tell me how it went for you. And as always, go check out gotmead.com for even more recipes, many by Rob.

See you around the mead world!

In Mead,
Vicky Rowe
Founder and Owner, Gotmead.com
Youngsville, NC
August 2017

INTRODUCTION

One of the most confusing tasks facing mead makers today is attempting to explain to their friends what exactly mead is. To be quite honest, we don't make it easy to do this. The fact that we have so many different types and categories of mead to choose from does little to simplify this task.

In this book I will address a style of mead known as the Melomel. A melomel is a type of mead made using honey with one or more fruit additions. Depending on the fruit base used, certain melomels may also be known by more specific sub-category names such as cyser, pyment, and morat. The term Melomel may have come originally from the Greek melomeli, literally "apple-honey" or "treefruit-honey".

Sub-categories of melomels also include Cysers and Pyments (See: Glossary of Terms). My ultimate goal here is to provide you, the reader, with a solid understanding of what Melomels are (or can be) and to provide you with enough examples that you will be able to very soon begin crafting your own recipes and fruit blends.

TYPES OF FRUIT

For the sake of reference, the following section will include an alphabetical selection of fruits along with a brief description of each. This is by no means a complete listing of all fruits available. It quickly becomes evident that a melomel is truly restricted only by the brewer's imagination and creative process.

Apple – (Fermentation points/lb. = 8; Approx. pH 3.30 – 4.00). With over 2,500 varieties grown in the United States and over 7,500 worldwide, apples are without a doubt the most popular of all fruits. They're generally available all year round and come in every flavor aspect you could want ranging from bitter to sour to sweet.

Apricot - (Fermentation points/lb. = 6; Approx. pH 3.30 – 4.80). Apricots are delicious when ripe. The fruit has only one seed, and the color runs from yellow to orange (possibly with a reddish cast), and the surface of the fruit is smooth and nearly hairless.

Blackberry - (Fermentation points/lb. = 3; Approx. pH 3.90 – 4.50). The blackberry has always grown in the wild and is a widespread genus. It also seems to be a native to many parts of the world.

Black Currant – (Fermentation points/lb. = 6; Approx. pH 2.6 – 3.1). Black Currants are a small, bitter-tasting fruit and are high in vitamin C. They can be found in central and northern Europe and northern Asia. Black Currant gets its name from its dark color.

Blueberry – (Fermentation points/lb. = 5; Approx. pH 3.11 – 3.22). A blueberry is a very small fruit. It grows in a small shrub. There are many types of blueberries growing in different regions of North America and eastern Asia. Blueberries have a sweet taste, with a little acidic hint. Wild blueberries have a stronger taste. Blueberries are typically most commonly found between May and October.

Boysenberry - (Fermentation points/lb. = 3; Approx. pH 3.00 – 3.50). A boysenberry is an aggregate fruit with large seeds and a maroon color. Boysenberries are a cross between a European raspberry, a common blackberry, an American dewberry, and a loganberry.

Cantaloupe Melon - (Fermentation points/lb. = 5; Approx. pH 6.00 – 6.60). Sometimes called a Rock Melon, the cantaloupe is a type of muskmelon. It was first cultivated in Italy and named after the city of Cantalupo. Canteloupe have a hard, scaly rind and are almost round in shape.

Cherry – (Fermentation points/lb. = 7; Approx. pH 3.25 – 4.54). A cherry is a fruit that grows on either a tree or a bush. It is usually red, with a seed in the middle. There are both sweet and sour varieties of cherry, but sour cherries are better for mead. Sweet cherries can give you a slightly "cough syrup-like" flavor in wines and meads.

Coconut – (Fermentation points/lb. = 4; Approx. pH 5.50 – 7.80). A coconut is a large nut from the Coconut Palm. The flesh of the coconut is white and can be eaten either raw or cooked. Lightly toasting coconut before using it in a wine or mead can help increase the flavor of this mild fruit/nut.

Cranberry – (Fermentation points/lb. = 3; Approx. pH 2.30 – 2.50). Grown primarily in the acidic bogs of the northern hemisphere, cranberries are a tart fruit that grow on low creeping dwarf shrubs that range at about 7' long and from 2"- 8" high.

Dragon fruit – (Fermentation points/lb. = 6; Approx. pH 4.00 – 5.00). Dragon fruit is a favorite to many. It has a light sweet taste, an intense shape and color, and a texture somewhere between a kiwi and an apple. Dragon fruit is typically grown in Central or South America and parts of Asia.

Elderberry - (Fermentation points/lb. = 4; Approx. pH 2.00 – 4.00). The black-berried elder complex is variously treated as a single species "Sambucus nigra" found in the warmer parts of Europe and North America with several regional varieties or subspecies. Ripe elderberries are actually poisonous so they should be slightly cooked before ingesting or using in wines or meads.

Gooseberry - (Fermentation points/lb. = 0; Approx. pH 2.80 – 3.10). Gooseberries are botanically a berry and a member of the same family as the currant. Some varieties are hairy and with colors ranging when ripe from green, white, yellow and red to almost black. All varieties can be picked young and cooked when green.

Grapes - (Fermentation points/lb. = 9; Approx. pH 2.80 – 3.82). Used for wine making for thousands of years, grapes come in red, purple, white, and green varieties. There are over 10,000 different varieties of grapes in the world.

Guava - (Fermentation points/lb. = 6; Approx. pH 3.37 – 4.10). These are delicious eaten raw while the whole fruit is edible. An average-sized guava contains about seven times the recommended daily intake of vitamin C.

Honeydew Melon - (Fermentation points/lb. = 5; Approx. pH 6.00 – 6.70). Honeydew, also known as Honey Melon, is a type of melon in the cultivar group muskmelon. Cucumis melo Inodorus group, which includes crenshaw, casaba, Persian, winter, and other mixed melons. When ripe, it is light, sweet, juicy, and very refreshing.

Kiwifruit – (Fermentation points/lb. = 6; Approx. pH 3.10 – 3.96). The kiwifruit is healthy and contains many vitamins and minerals. Kiwis are rich in vitamin C, vitamin K, potassium, and fiber. They also provide more vitamin C than an equivalent amount of orange.

Kumquat - (Fermentation points/lb. = 6; Approx. pH 3.64 – 4.25). Kumquats are often preserved in sweet syrup and used for marmalade and garnishes, but fresh ones are delicious in fruit salads or for eating just as they are.

Lemon - (Fermentation points/lb. = 2; Approx. pH 2.00 – 2.60). The lemon is the common name for "Citrus Limon". It is a yellow citrus fruit related to the orange. Lemon juice is about 5% citric acid, and has a pH of 2 to 3. This gives lemons their sour taste. The juice, zest, and pulp are often used in cooking.

Lime - (Fermentation points/lb. = 1; Approx. pH 2.00 – 2.80). Limes are only green because they are picked unripe but if left to ripen they turn yellow. Limes can be used like lemons but as their juice is more acidic, less lime is typically needed.

Mandarin/Tangerine - (Fermentation points/lb. = 7; Approx. pH 3.30 – 4.34). Mandarins are a citrus fruit that is a variety of orange and are usually eaten either as part of a fruit salad or by themselves. Mandarins are easily peeled with your fingers and they can be easily split into even segments without squirting juice all over the place.

Mango - (Fermentation points/lb. = 9; Approx. pH 3.40 – 4.80). Mangoes grow in many tropical climates worldwide, the fruit ranges in color from green to golden yellow and orange-red, and its flesh is a juicy, deep orange surrounding a large flat inedible stone. Mangoes also make excellent ice creams, sorbets, sauces and drinks like smoothies.

Marionberry – (Fermentation points/lb. = 1; Approx. pH 2.80 – 3.80). A type of blackberry developed in the northwestern region of North America.

Mulberry – (Fermentation points/lb. = 5; Approx. pH 3.37 – 5.33.) Native to the warm regions of Asia, Africa, and the Americas, mulberries are a type of tree. The fruit of the Black Mulberry (Southwest Asia) and the Red Mulberry (North America) have the strongest flavors. The fruit of the White Mulberry (East Asia) species has a very weak flavor.

Nectarine - (Fermentation points/lb. = 5; Approx. pH 3.92 – 4.18). The nectarine flesh is rich, sweet and juicy and is well suited for eating fresh and for using in ice cream, pies and fruit salads. Color can range from silvery white or yellowy orange to pinkish red. While often described as a cross between a peach and a plum, nectarines are actually a variety of smooth-skinned peach.

Orange - (Fermentation points/lb. = 6; Approx. pH 3.30 – 4.34). Oranges are best eaten in their natural state but can be used in variety of desserts, pastries, fruit salads, mousses, soufflés, ice creams and sorbets. It can be squeezed for juice or used to marinate poultry or fish. Oranges fall into two groups: sweet oranges, which can be eaten raw, and bitter oranges, which cannot be eaten raw, but are used for making marmalade, jams, and jellies instead. With its citrusy flavor, orange juice (or zest) can make a great addition to a mead.

Papaya - (Fermentation points/lb. = 5; Approx. pH 5.20 – 6.00). A papaya is a large tropical fruit whose ripe flesh can be juicy, creamy, orange-red, or yellow. In the center is a mass of large peppery black seeds, which are edible and sometimes crushed and used as a spice.

Passion fruit – (Fermentation points/lb. = 7; Approx. pH 2.70 – 3.30). Passion fruit is a highly fragrant, sweet, but slightly tart, tasting fruit that can be spooned out and eaten fresh or added to fruit salad. It is most commonly found being used in drinks, ice creams and sorbets, or as a flavoring for many types of desserts.

Peaches - (Fermentation points/lb. = 6; Approx. pH 3.30 – 4.05). Peaches are a type of "stone fruit" because they have a shell of hard wood around their seed, called a stone or a pit. The skin of a peach can have an orange or yellow color, and it is covered in small hairs called peach fuzz. The inside of a peach ranges in color from white to golden depending on the variety.

Pear - (Fermentation points/lb. = 6; Approx. pH 3.50 – 4.60). Pears contain a small amount of vitamin A & C and some potassium and riboflavin. They normally come in a teardrop shape and can be canned, frozen, or eaten fresh.

Persimmon - (Fermentation points/lb. = 8; Approx. pH 4.42 – 4.70). Originally from Japan, persimmons are now widely grown in all parts of the world. Resembling a tomato in appearance, the fruit is round and smooth-skinned, changing from yellow to red when it ripens.

Pineapple – (Fermentation points/lb. = 8; Approx. pH 3.20 – 4.00). Native to South America, Central America and the Caribbean, pineapples have a juicy, sweet-but sometimes slightly tart-fragrant flavor.

Plum - (Fermentation points/lb. = 6; Approx. pH 2.80 – 4.30). A plum is a sweet type of stone fruit. They can be yellow, red, green or even white. The flesh of the fruit is brownish and is very juicy and the skin can be eaten.

Pomegranate - (Fermentation points/lb. = 9; Approx. pH 2.93 – 3.20). An exotic-looking fruit about the size of a large apple with a thin, tough skin (usually golden to deep red), pomegranates are filled with edible seeds surrounded by a crimson-colored pulp. Once separated from the fruit, the tangy sweet seeds are eaten fresh, added to salads, or pressed to extract their juice.

Raspberry – (Fermentation points/lb. = 3; Approx. pH 3.22 – 3.95). Raspberries are typically harvested when the fruit comes off the receptacle easily and have turned a deep color (red, black, purple, or golden yellow, depending on the type). This is when the fruits are ripest and sweetest.

Red Currant – (Fermentation points/lb. = 4; Approx. pH 2.5 – 3.2). Red Currants are a type of fruit related to the Black Currants. They can be found primarily in Western Europe.

Star Fruit – (Fermentation points/lb. = 3; Approx. pH 3.80 – 4.10). Star Fruit is found primarily in India, Indonesia, and Sri Lanka. Star fruit is also common in the south of Asia, Australia and all of the islands around Australia. It tastes best when ripe (yellow with a bit of green). When ripe, the edges will feel a bit hard and will be slightly brown.

Strawberry - (Fermentation points/lb. = 4; Approx. pH 3.00 – 3.90). A unique fruit, the seeds grow around the outside of the fruit rather than inside it. Strawberries come in many different varieties.

Tamarind - (Fermentation points/lb. = 36; Approx. pH 3.00 – 3.20). Tamarind is a kind of tree in the Fabaceae family. It is found in Africa primarily the Sudan.

Watermelon - (Fermentation points/lb. = 6; Approx. pH 5.18 – 5.60). The high water content of watermelons means that they are low in calories. They contain some vitamins B and C. Watermelon is excellent juiced, chopped up into a fruit salad, or just eaten in chunky slices. Yeast (Brands, Strains, Characteristics)

YEAST (Brands, Strains, & Characteristics)

Another item that has many available choices to a mead maker is which type of yeast to use. Most of us have our favorites of course, but the best yeast to use for a particular type of mead can definitely vary from recipe to recipe. Some are better for "Traditionals" and some are better for fruit meads or "Melomels". In the end however, the best yeast for any given mead is going to be the one you prefer the most for each recipe you develop.

The main wine yeast suppliers typically used by home brewers in North America are Red Star, Lalvin, Wyeast, and White Star types. The following is a listing of the yeast strains used in this book. My personal preferences tend toward Lalvin strains but admittedly, that's because they are normally easier to acquire than some others.

RC-212: Dark Grape Pyments
- Fermentation Range: 59-86F; ABV Tolerance: 14%
- Ideal for full-bodied red wines. Emphasizes fruit and spice notes, accentuates character in red grapes.

ICV-D47: Citrus or Tropical Fruit based melomels
- Fermentation Range: 50-95F; ABV Tolerance: 15%
- Leaves a wine very full bodied with enhanced mouthfeel. Accentuates varietal character and contributes ripe tropical fruit and citrus notes.

71B-1122: Berry Melomels
- Fermentation Range: 59-86F; ABV Tolerance: 14%
- Semi-dry white wine yeast that will enhance fruit flavors and adds fruity esters. Can be used with whites, rosés, nouveaus, and concentrates.

K1V-1116: Cysers (although ICV-D47 will also work well)

- Fermentation Range: 50-107F; ABV Tolerance: 18%
- A vigorous and competitive fermenter that, because of its neutral effect on varietal character, is very well suited to fruit wines as well as wines to be made from.

EC-1118 (Bayanus): Polish Trójniaks, dark fruit
- Fermentation Range: 50-86F; ABV Tolerance: 18%
- This strain has a strong competitive character, the ability to ferment at low temperature, good flocculation, and an excellent alcohol tolerance.
- Used in a wide range of applications (such as sparkling wines, fruit wines and ciders).
- Leaves a wine very full bodied with enhanced mouthfeel.
- Accentuates varietal character and contributes ripe tropical fruit and citrus notes.

Fermivin PDM: Polish Trójniaks, dark fruit
- Fermentation Range: 55-86F; ABV Tolerance: 16%
- A rapid and complete fermenter, clean finish that lets this yeast work very well for white, pink, or sparkling wines.

Fermicru VR5: Polish Trójniaks, dark fruit
- Fermentation Range: 65-86F; ABV Tolerance: 15.5%
- Ideally suited to the production red wines for aging.
- Strengthens the structure, body and aromatic finesse of major red grape varieties
- Develops fruity aromas (ie: blackcurrant and cherries)
- Works very with red or dark fruit wines for aging.

Enovini WS: Polish Trójniaks, dark fruit
- Fermentation Range: 59-86F; ABV Tolerance: 13%
- Used for making white, pink and red house wines. Recommended fermentation temperature 15 - 30 ° C.
- Used to obtain mature dry, semi-dry or even semi-sweet wines without the risk of further fermentation in bottles. This type of wine yeast produces a mild, balanced wine with a clearer fruit note.

SWEETNESS LEVELS

The actual level of sweetness in your mead can be as varied as you'd like them to be. Contrary to popular opinion, mead is not always a sickly sweet beverage. Great meads range from the traditional dessert sweet meads to the driest possible meads you can find or make. It all comes down to your preferences and imagination. The following is a basic description of each level of sweetness and what the specific gravity range of each would be.

- Dry: 0.998 – 1.010
- Semisweet: 1.011 – 1.020
- Sweet: 1.021 – 1.030
- Dessert: 1.031 and higher

CALCULATING ABV (Specific Gravity & Brix)

The alcohol content of your mead will typically be measured in one of two ways. You'll either use calculations based on the Specific Gravity of your must, or you'll use calculations based on the Brix.

Specific gravity is the ratio of the density of a substance to the density of a reference substance; equivalently, it is the ratio of the mass of a substance to the mass of a reference substance for the same given volume.

- ABV = (OG – FG) * 131.25

Degrees Brix (symbol °Bx) is the sugar content of an aqueous solution. For every gram of sugar that is converted during fermentation, about half a gram of alcohol is produced.

- Brix = 261.3 * (1 - 1 / Specific Gravity) Specific Gravity = 261.3 / (Brix / 261.3)

NUTRIENTS (Types and their use)

In regard to home brewing meads, nutrients can be defined as pretty much anything your yeast need to survive during the fermentation process. This can range from food, vitamins, chemicals, air, or anything else that lessens the stress on the yeast while it works its magic changing the must into mead.

Typically, nutrients will involve one of more of the following depending on several factors.

- Diammonium Phosphate (DAP): Contains fermentable nitrogen (N) at 25g/HL.
- Go Ferm: Contains micronutrients to feed your yeast and allow them to create healthy cells. Very effective in high alcohol situations.
- Fermax: Contains Diammonium Phosphate, dipotassium phosphate, magnesium sulfate & autolyzed yeast.
- Fermaid: Also known as Fermaid-K or Fermaid-O. Contains amino acids, sterols, yeast hulls, vitamins & a limited amount of fermentable nitrogen
- Yeast Hulls: The cell walls of the hulls absorb auto toxic yeast byproducts that could inhibit alcoholic and malolactic fermentations. You would use yeast hulls by themselves if you encountered a stuck (or sluggish) fermentation.

TAILORED ORGANIC STAGGERED NUTRIENT ADDITIONS

TOSNA 2.0

The TOSNA protocol has been refined and simplified after real world use in the commercial mead scene with guidance from one of the leading authorities in the wine industry today, Scott Laboratories. It has been tailored even further, taking yeast selection into consideration now as well.

Initial Sugar (g/L) x N requirement factor / 50 (ppm) x batch size (gals) = Total Fermaid-O (grams)

Sugar (g/L)
Brix x 10 = Sugar (g/L)
*1° Brix ≈ 10 g/L sugar

Nitrogen (N) Requirement Factor
- For Low N requiring strains, Sugar (g/L) x 0.75 = YAN requirement
- For Medium N requiring strains, Sugar (g/L) x 0.90 = YAN requirement
- For High N requiring strains, Sugar (g/L) x 1.25 = YAN requirement

*Sugar (g/L) = Brix x 10
*Factors sourced from Scott Labs fermentation handbook 2016

- Common yeasts w/ Low N needs, 71B, DV10, D47, EC1118
- Common yeasts w/ Medium N needs, D21, D254, D80, V1116
- Common yeasts w/ High Nitrogen needs, CY3079, RC212

*Information on additional yeast strains can be found on Lallemand's website.

50 (ppm) Effectiveness using Fermaid-O
1g/gal of Fermaid-O = 50ppm (or mg) of N/L effectiveness
*It is recommended to invest in a good grams scale

NUTRIENT ADDITION SCHEDULE

Once you get your total Fermaid-O to be used based on the TOSNA formula above, you can divide the total by 4 to get the grams of each individual nutrient addition you will be adding, as follows:

- The first three nutrient additions are added at 24, 48, and 72 hours after pitching the yeast.
- The final nutrient addition is on Day 7, or when fermentation reaches the 1/3 sugar break.

NOTE *When fermenting with fruit and/or fruit juice, the amount of Fermaid-O can be cut by half.*

BJCP CATEGORIES (Beer Judge Certification Program)

The BJCP is a non-profit organization that certifies and ranks beer judges. Recently they've added a certification for Mead Judge to provide accurate, standardized judging for meads and cysers via sub-dividing them into specific categories for proper classification.

The BJCP currently categorizes competitive meads into 19 defined categories. While this provides a great foundation for judging meads competitively, there will be a need for further classifications and sub-categories to be created in the future. As this is a book covering the various types of Melomels, the BJCP categories I'll be covering will include the following groups…

M2A – Cyser - A blend of honey and apple juice fermented together.

M2B – Pyment – a blend honey and red (or white) grapes. Pyment made with white grape juice is sometimes called "white mead".

M2C – Berry – A berry can be defined as a pulpy and usually edible fruit (i.e.: strawberry, raspberry, or blueberry) of small size irrespective of its structure.

M2D – Stone Fruit - A "Stone Fruit" melomel is any melomel made using a fruit that has a stone-like pit at its core. Examples of this could be cherries, peaches, plums, etc.

M2E – Other/Mixed Fruit - This type of melomel uses any fruit not considered a berry or any blend of multiple fruits to layer different flavors together. Some of the most complex meads I've come across have been in this category

M4B – Historical/Indigenous - "Historical Mead" is any historically reproduced mead or an indigenous type of mead to a certain region that doesn't fit into another subcategory (e.g., Ethiopian Tej, Polish meads, etc.).

EQUIPMENT LIST

The following is a fairly basic list of equipment you'll need to create most of the meads listed in the next section. Prices listed for each piece are approximate but should be fairly close to what you'll pay either online or in your local Home Brew Store. You don't actually need everything I've listed to replicate the recipes in this book, but it will definitely make things easier for you in the long run if you purchase most (or all) of them. I did.

Airlock (3-piece, plastic)	$1.69
Auto-siphon	$9.99
Brewing Thermometer	$6.99
Clear Vinyl Tubing	$0.49/ft.
Funnel (4" diameter)	$3.99
Glass Carboy (1 gallon)	$5.99
Glass Carboy (5 gallon)	$44.99
Hydrometer	$6.99
Incremental Gram Scale	$50.00
Plastic Brewing Bucket (2 gallon)	$12.48
Plastic Brewing Bucket (6 gallon)	$12.99
Refractometer	$59.99
Racking Cane	$3.99
Stainless Steel Fruit Press (3-liter)	$112.99
Double Sieve (10" diameter)	$36.99
#6 Rubber Plug (w/hole for airlocks)	$1.39

At a bare minimum, you'll want to at least buy the equipment listed here.

Airlock (3-piece, plastic)	$1.69
Auto-siphon	$9.99
Brewing Thermometer	$6.99
Clear Vinyl Tubing	$0.49/ft.
Funnel (4" diameter)	$3.99
Glass Carboy (1 gallon)	$5.99
Hydrometer	$6.99
Plastic Brewing Bucket (2 gallon)	$12.48
Double Sieve (10" diameter)	$36.99
Rubber Plug (w/hole for airlocks)	$1.50

READING A HYDROMETER

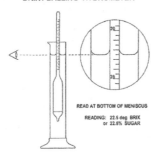

READ AT BOTTOM OF MENISCUS

READING: 22.5 deg BRIX
or 22.5% SUGAR

Hydrometers are a tool that every home brewer and wine maker should become familiar with because they can tell you so much about what is going on, like how close your mead is to being done. A hydrometer is a glass tube with a weight on one end. Its purpose is to measure the difference in gravity (density) between pure water and water with sugar dissolved in it. The hydrometer takes this reading by floating in the liquid.

It is best to use a hydrometer test jar to take your samples. Test jars are made of plastic or glass and allow you to take a small sample to be tested. Newer winemakers and brewers tend to take a lot of samples (and so do us 'old timers'!). Try not to sample too much, for a couple reasons:

- You want to have mead left over to drink at the end!
- Each time you sample you introduce the possibility of infection

Honestly, you really only need to take samples at the beginning when you pitch your mead, at the first break (when the hydrometer readings have moved 1/3 of the way from where you started to where you want to finish), and each time you rack. And of course when you bottle.

Today, once everything starts fermenting, you have very little to worry about. Keep in mind that every time you open your fermenter you are allowing the possibility for bacteria to be introduced.

Use a turkey baster or wine thief to take your samples. And of course, make sure everything is sanitized before use. On most of the hydrometers made today you have three scales for taking measurements. The three scales are potential alcohol, Balling, and specific gravity. Which scale you use will depend on how specific you want your reading to be. The easiest scale to use is the potential alcohol.

How to take a hydrometer reading using the potential alcohol scale:

- Sanitize all equipment that will come in contact with your wine or beer.
- Take a sample of the liquid before you add the yeast.
- Place the sample in the hydrometer test jar.
- Place the hydrometer in the test jar. Make sure the hydrometer is not hitting the sides of the jar as this will affect your reading.
- Spin the hydrometer as you would a top to remove any bubbles that might be clinging to it.
- With the sample at eye level, look to see where the liquid crosses the markings.
- Write down the reading. (Hopefully you're taking notes about all your measurements and mead creating activities)
- Let the beer or wine ferment completely. You'll know it's done when you see one bubble a minute or less coming out of the airlock.
- Take a second reading just before bottling.
- To determine the amount of alcohol you subtract the second reading from the first. For example if your first reading was 5% and your second reading is 1%; take 5-1=4%. That is the amount of alcohol.

Links in this chapter:
- Hydrometer - http://bit.ly/2m5hPBq
- Hydrometer test jar - http://bit.ly/2lsfQny
- Wine Thief - http://bit.ly/2lkapZn

UNIT CONVERSIONS (US to Metric)

Fluid Conversions

1 Gallon	=	3.79 liters
33.81 Fluid Ounce	=	1 liter
5 gallons	=	18.93 liters
5.28 gallons	=	20 liters
1 fluid ounce	=	29.58 milliliters
1 cup	=	240 milliliters
0.03 fluid ounces	=	1 milliliter
1 tablespoon	=	14.79 milliliters

Mass Conversions

1 pound	=	0.45 kilograms
1 ounce	=	28.35 grams
2.20 pounds	=	1 kilogram
0.04 ounces	=	1 gram

CALCULATIONS & FORMULAS

Fermentation Equation: Converts sugar into Alcohol and Carbon Dioxide

$$C_6H_{12}O_6 = 2\ C_2H_5OH + 2\ CO_2$$

Alcohol by Volume (ABV)

$$ABV = (OG - FG) * 131.25$$

Converting Specific Gravity to Brix

$$Brix = (((182.4601 * SG\ \text{-}775.6821) * SG\ \text{+}1262.7794) * SG\ \text{-}669.5622)$$

Converting Brix to Specific Gravity

$$SG = (Brix\ /\ (258.6\text{-}((Brix\ /\ 258.2)*227.1))) + 1$$

Sugar (g/L)

Brix x 10 = Sugar (g/L)

TOSNA for Low Nitrogen requiring yeast strains

Sugar (g/L) x 0.75 = YAN requirement

TOSNA for Medium Nitrogen requiring yeast strains

For Medium N requiring strains, Sugar (g/L) x 0.90 = YAN Requirement

TOSNA for High Nitrogen requiring yeast strains

For High N requiring strains, Sugar (g/L) x 1.25 = YAN Requirement

RECIPES

Considering that most of my favorite meads tend to lean toward Melomels of different types, it will come as no surprise that we are now getting to my favorite part of this book. The following is a selection of my favorite fruit mead recipes. Some of them are proven recipes and some are conceptual, but all of them will produce good meads.

M2A – Cysers (Apple Meads)
- Oaked Orange Blossom
- Simple "Dry" Cyser
- Simple "Semi-Sweet" Cyser
- Simple "Sweet" Cyser
- Simple "Dessert/Sack" Cyser

M2B – Pyments (Grape Meads)
- Concord Grape
- Muscadine Grape
- White Grape

M2C – Berry Meads
- Black Currant (Black Mead)
- Blackberry
- Blueberry
- Cranberry
- Raspberry
- Strawberry

M2D – Stone Fruit Meads
- Cherry (Sour)
- Mango

M2E - Other/Mixed Fruit
- Apple-Blackberry
- Apple-Blueberry-Cranberry
- Apple-Blueberry
- Apple-Cranberry
- Apple-Raspberry
- Apple-Sour Cherry
- Black Currant-Blueberry-Blackberry
- Blueberry-Blackberry-Raspberry-Sour Cherry

- Blackberry-Blueberry
- Blueberry - Black Currant
- Blackberry-Blueberry-Raspberry-Sour Cherry
- Blueberry-Blackberry-Raspberry-Strawberry-Sour Cherry
- Blueberry-Blackberry-Raspberry-Strawberry
- Coconut
- Cranberry-Raspberry
- Elderberry-Blackberry
- Orange- Mango
- Orange-Pineapple-Coconut
- Orange-Pineapple
- Orange-Raspberry
- Pineapple-Sour Cherry
- Pineapple
- Pineapple-Mango
- Strawberry-Kiwi

M4B – Historical/Indigenous (Polish Melomels)

- Trójniak 26   2nd Place – MCI 2012
- Trójniak 41   2nd Place – MCI 2013
- Trójniak 43   2nd Place – MCI 2014
- Trójniak 54   3rd Place – MCI 2015
- Trójniak 64   3rd Place – MFoD 2015 (Mead Free or Die)
- Trójniak 83   1st Place – Valhalla 2016
- Trójniak 102   3rd Place – MCI 2016
- Trójniak 103 "Sofia"   Best of Show – Texas Mead Fest 2016
- Trójniak 104   3rd Place – MFoD 2016
- Trójniak 108   3rd Place – MCI 2017; 2nd Place - MFoD 2017
- Trójniak 109
- Trójniak 114   1st Place – Domras Cup 2017
- Trójniak 117
- Trójniak 121   2nd Place – MFoD 2017
- Trójniak 134
- Trójniak Agrestniak
- Trójniak Smorodyniak
- Trójniak Wiśniak z Czeremchą
- Trójniak Wiśniak
- Dwójniak Aroniak   Best of Show – MFoD 2016

M2A – Cysers (Apple Meads)

A good Cyser combines a blend of one or more types of fresh pressed apple juice combined with honey and yeast and then fermented to a nice crisp finish. It can run any level of sweetness although I prefer a border between dry and Semi-Sweet myself to capture that fresh, crisp, apple aspect reminiscent of an autumn afternoon at a local orchard.

Oaked Orange Blossom Cyser

Yield: 1 gallon   OG: 1.106   FG: 1.015   ABV: 12%
Starting Brix: 25.17   Final Brix: 3.83

Primary
Unfiltered Apple Juice: 1 gallon
Yeast: 2 grams, Lalvin, D-47
GoFerm: 2.50 grams
Nutrients: 1.89 grams Fermaid-O (0.47 grams each at 24, 48, 72 hours after pitching yeast. 4th dose to be administered at either the 1/3 sugar break or on 7th day)
Pectic Enzyme: per manufacturer's direction
Orange Blossom Honey: 1.76 lbs.

Secondary
Sodium Metabisuphite and Potassium Sorbate (per manufacturer's direction)
American Oak Cubes, Medium Toast: 5-6 cubes for 1 month

Final Racking
Rack mead one final time and let it sit until the mead is clear enough to read through. (Bulk age until ready to bottle)

Directions:
- Before starting, clean and sanitize all of your equipment

Must Preparation
- Pour 2 quarts of apple juice into a large stock pot and bring to a low boil
- Remove from the heat and blend in the honey, stirring until it is completely dissolved
- Add additional juice to bring total volume to 1 gallon
- Allow must to cool to room temperature then take a gravity reading
- Pour the cooled must into a 2 gallon brewing bucket and cover with a sanitary cloth and a large rubber band

Yeast Starter
- Mix GoFerm with 50 ml of hot water
- Allow mixture to cool to 104F then add your yeast and stir until dissolved
- Let this mixture sit for 15-20 minutes to allow it to activate and grow into a nice healthy colony

Primary
- When the temperature of the yeast starter drops to within 10 degrees of the must, pour it into the primary bucket and stir it thoroughly to disperse
- Add nutrients (Fermaid-O) as directed above
- Add Pectic Enzyme: per manufacturer's direction
- Aerate must twice daily until 1/3 sugar break then once daily until 2/3 sugar break
- When OG reaches target FG, rack to secondary

Secondary
- Rack primary must into a clean glass carboy over Sodium Metabisuphite and Potassium Sorbate to kill any remaining yeast and leave most of the sediment behind.
- Add Oak Cubes, an airlock, & set aside for 1 month

Final Racking
- Rack mead one final time and let it sit until the mead is clear enough to read through (Bulk age until ready to bottle)

Simple "Dry" Cyser

Yield: 1 gallon   OG: 1.081   FG: 1.005   ABV: 12%
Starting Brix: 19.65   Final Brix: 1.28

Primary
Unfiltered Apple Juice: 1 gallon
Yeast: 1 gram, Lalvin, D-47
GoFerm: 1.25 grams
Nutrients: 2.95 grams Fermaid-O (0.74 grams each at 24, 48, 72 hours after pitching yeast. 4th dose to be administered at either the 1/3 sugar break or on 7th day)
Acid Blend: 4 grams
Pectic Enzyme: per manufacturer's direction
Wildflower Honey: 1.04 lbs.

Secondary
Sodium Metabisuphite and Potassium Sorbate (per manufacturer's direction)

Final Racking
Rack mead one final time and let it sit until the mead is clear enough to read through. (Bulk age until ready to bottle)

Directions:
- Before starting, clean and sanitize all of your equipment.

Must Preparation
- Pour 2 quarts of apple juice into a large stock pot and bring to a low boil
- Remove from the heat and blend in the honey, stirring until it is completely dissolved
- Add additional juice to bring total volume to 1 gallon
- Allow must to cool to room temperature then take a gravity reading
- Pour the cooled must into a 2 gallon brewing bucket and cover with a sanitary cloth and a large rubber band

Yeast Starter
- Mix GoFerm with 25 ml of hot water
- Allow mixture to cool to 104F then add your yeast and stir until dissolved
- Let this mixture sit for 15-20 minutes to allow it to activate and grow into a nice healthy colony

Primary
- When the temperature of the yeast starter drops to within 10 degrees of the must, pour it into the primary bucket and stir it thoroughly to disperse
- Add nutrients (Fermaid-O) as directed above
- Add Acid Blend: 4 grams
- Add Pectic Enzyme: per manufacturer's direction
- Aerate must twice daily until 1/3 sugar break then once daily until 2/3 sugar break
- When SG reaches target FG, rack to secondary

Secondary
- Rack primary must into a clean glass carboy over Sodium Metabisuphite and Potassium Sorbate to kill any remaining yeast and leave most of the sediment behind
- Add an airlock.
- Leave in secondary until it clears

Final Racking
- Rack mead one final time and let it sit until the mead is clear enough to read through (Bulk age until ready to bottle)

Simple "Semi-Sweet" Cyser

Yield: 1 gallon   OG: 1.091   FG: 1.015   ABV: 12%
Starting Brix: 21.89   Final Brix: 3.83

Primary

Unfiltered Apple Juice: 1 gallon
Yeast: 1 gram, Lalvin, D-47
GoFerm: 1.25 grams
Nutrients: 3.28 grams Fermaid-O (0.82 grams each at 24, 48, 72 hours after pitching yeast. 4th dose to be administered at either the 1/3 sugar break or on 7th day)
Acid Blend: 4 grams
Pectic Enzyme: per manufacturer's direction
Wildflower Honey: 1.33 lbs.

Secondary

Sodium Metabisuphite and Potassium Sorbate (per manufacturer's direction)

Final Racking

Rack mead one final time and let it sit until the mead is clear enough to read through. (Bulk age until ready to bottle)

Directions:

-   Before starting, clean and sanitize all of your equipment.

Must Preparation

-   Pour 2 quarts of apple juice into a large stock pot and bring to a low boil
-   Remove from the heat and blend in the honey, stirring until it is completely dissolved
-   Add additional juice to bring total volume to 1 gallon
-   Allow must to cool to room temperature then take a gravity reading
-   Pour the cooled must into a 2 gallon brewing bucket and cover with a sanitary cloth and a large rubber band

Yeast Starter

-   Mix GoFerm with 25 ml of hot water
-   Allow mixture to cool to 104F then add your yeast and stir until dissolved
-   Let this mixture sit for 15-20 minutes to allow it to activate and grow into a nice healthy colony

Primary

-   When the temperature of the yeast starter drops to within 10 degrees of the must, pour it into the primary bucket and stir it thoroughly to disperse
-   Add nutrients (Fermaid-O) as directed above
-   Add Acid Blend: 4 grams
-   Add Pectic Enzyme: per manufacturer's direction
-   Aerate must twice daily until 1/3 sugar break then once daily until 2/3 sugar break
-   When SG reaches target FG, rack to secondary

Secondary

-   Rack primary must into a clean glass carboy over Sodium Metabisuphite and Potassium Sorbate to kill any remaining yeast and leave most of the sediment behind
-   Add an airlock.
-   Leave in secondary until it clears

Final Racking

-   Rack mead one final time and let it sit until the mead is clear enough to read through (Bulk age until ready to bottle)

Simple "Sweet" Cyser

Yield: 1 gallon   OG: 1.117   FG: 1.025   ABV: 14%
Starting Brix: 27.37   Final Brix: 6.33

Primary
Unfiltered Apple Juice: 1 gallon
Yeast: 1 gram, Lalvin, D-47
GoFerm: 1.25 grams
Nutrients: 4.11 grams Fermaid-O (1.03 grams each at 24, 48, 72 hours after pitching yeast. 4th dose to be administered at either the 1/3 sugar break or on 7th day)
Acid Blend: 4 grams
Pectic Enzyme: per manufacturer's direction
Wildflower Honey: 2.05 lbs.

Secondary
Sodium Metabisuphite and Potassium Sorbate (per manufacturer's direction)

Final Racking
Rack mead one final time and let it sit until the mead is clear enough to read through. (Bulk age until ready to bottle)

Directions:
- Before starting, clean and sanitize all of your equipment.

Must Preparation
- Pour 2 quarts of apple juice into a large stock pot and bring to a low boil
- Remove from the heat and blend in the honey, stirring until it is completely dissolved
- Add additional juice to bring total volume to 1 gallon
- Allow must to cool to room temperature then take a gravity reading
- Pour the cooled must into a 2 gallon brewing bucket and cover with a sanitary cloth and a large rubber band

Yeast Starter
- Mix GoFerm with 25 ml of hot water
- Allow mixture to cool to 104F then add your yeast and stir until dissolved
- Let this mixture sit for 15-20 minutes to allow it to activate and grow into a nice healthy colony

Primary
- When the temperature of the yeast starter drops to within 10 degrees of the must, pour it into the primary bucket and stir it thoroughly to disperse
- Add nutrients (Fermaid-O) as directed above
- Add Acid Blend: 4 grams
- Add Pectic Enzyme: per manufacturer's direction
- Aerate must twice daily until 1/3 sugar break then once daily until 2/3 sugar break
- When OG reaches target FG, rack to secondary

Secondary
- Rack primary must into a clean glass carboy over Sodium Metabisuphite and Potassium Sorbate to kill any remaining yeast and leave most of the sediment behind
- Add an airlock.
- Leave in secondary until it clears

Final Racking
- Rack mead one final time and let it sit until the mead is clear enough to read through (Bulk age until ready to bottle)

Simple "Dessert/Sack" Cyser

Yield: 1 gallon   OG: 1.142   FG: 1.035   ABV: 16%
Starting Brix: 32.64   Final Brix: 8.78

Primary

Unfiltered Apple Juice: 1 gallon
Yeast: 1 gram, Lalvin, K1V-1116
GoFerm: 1.25 grams
Nutrients: 4.90 grams Fermaid-O (1.22 grams each at 24, 48, 72 hours after pitching yeast. 4th dose to be administered at either the 1/3 sugar break or on 7th day)
Acid Blend: 4 grams
Pectic Enzyme: per manufacturer's direction
Wildflower Honey: 2.77 lbs.

Secondary

Sodium Metabisuphite and Potassium Sorbate (per manufacturer's direction)

Final Racking

Rack mead one final time and let it sit until the mead is clear enough to read through. (Bulk age until ready to bottle)

"LET THERE BE MELOMELS!" BY ROBERT RATLIFF

Directions:
- Before starting, clean and sanitize all of your equipment.

Must Preparation
- Pour 2 quarts of apple juice into a large stock pot and bring to a low boil
- Remove from the heat and blend in the honey, stirring until it is completely dissolved
- Add additional juice to bring total volume to 1 gallon
- Allow must to cool to room temperature then take a gravity reading
- Pour the cooled must into a 2 gallon brewing bucket and cover with a sanitary cloth and a large rubber band

Yeast Starter
- Mix GoFerm with 25 ml of hot water
- Allow mixture to cool to 104F then add your yeast and stir until dissolved
- Let this mixture sit for 15-20 minutes to allow it to activate and grow into a nice healthy colony

Primary
- When the temperature of the yeast starter drops to within 10 degrees of the must, pour it into the primary bucket and stir it thoroughly to disperse
- Add nutrients (Fermaid-O) as directed above
- Add Acid Blend: 4 grams
- Add Pectic Enzyme: per manufacturer's direction
- Aerate must twice daily until 1/3 sugar break then once daily until 2/3 sugar break
- When SG reaches target FG, rack to secondary

Secondary
- Rack primary must into a clean glass carboy over Sodium Metabisuphite and Potassium Sorbate to kill any remaining yeast and leave most of the sediment behind
- Add an airlock.
- Leave in secondary until it clears

Final Racking
- Rack mead one final time and let it sit until the mead is clear enough to read through (Bulk age until ready to bottle)

M2B – Pyments (Grape Meads)

Pyments are a great option for lovers of both wine and mead. Some call them a 'gateway mead', because of their appeal to both groups. They use honey as their primary sugar source, but also incorporate one or more grape blends to combine in a wonderful combination of the two.

Pyments can come in any level of sweetness and also bring a nice tannic or acid finish to the mead depending on what types of grapes are used.

Concord Pyment "Semi-Sweet" Grape Mead

Yield: 1 gallon   OG: 1.106   FG: 1.015   ABV: 12%
Starting Brix: 25.17   Final Brix: 3.83

Primary

Yeast: 2 grams, Red Star, Montrachet
GoFerm: 2.50 grams
Nutrients: 6 grams Fermaid-O (1.5 grams each at 24, 48, 72 hours after pitching yeast. 4th dose to be administered at either the 1/3 sugar break or on 7th day)
Wildflower Honey: 2.6 lbs.
Welch's 100% Concord Grape Juice: 2 cans
Pectic Enzyme: per manufacturer's direction

Secondary

Sodium Metabisuphite and Potassium Sorbate (per manufacturer's directions)
Let sit at cellar or room temperature until clear

Final Racking

Rack mead one final time and let it sit until the mead is clear enough to read through. (Bulk age until ready to bottle)

Directions:
- Before starting, clean and sanitize all of your equipment

Must Preparation
- Pour concentrated grape juice into a clean glass, or Pyrex, measuring cup.
- Pour 6 cans of water into a large stockpot and bring to a low boil.
- Remove from the heat and blend in the honey, stirring until it is completely dissolved.
- Add the frozen juice and stir until thoroughly blended.
- Add additional water to bring total liquid volume to 1 gallon
- Allow must to cool to room temperature then take a gravity reading.
- Adjust gravity to Brix 25.17 by adding more honey or water as needed.
- Pour the cooled must into a 2 gallon brewing bucket and cover with a sanitary cloth and a large rubber band

Yeast Starter
- Mix 2.5 ml GoFerm with 50 ml of boiling water and 2 grams of sugar.
- Allow mixture to cool to 104F then add your yeast and stir until well dispersed.
- Let this mixture sit for 15-20 minutes to allow it to activate and grow into a nice healthy colony

Primary
- When the temperature of the yeast starter drops to within 10 degrees of the must, pour it into the primary bucket and stir it thoroughly to disperse.
- Add nutrients (Fermaid-O) as directed above.
- Add Pectic Enzyme: per manufacturer's direction
- Aerate must twice daily until 1/3 sugar break then once daily until 2/3 sugar break.
- When OG reaches target FG, rack to secondary.

Secondary
- Rack primary must into a clean glass carboy over Sodium Metabisuphite and Potassium Sorbate to kill any remaining yeast and leave most of the sediment behind
- Add an airlock
- Leave in secondary until it clears

Final Racking
- Rack mead one final time and let it sit until the mead is clear enough to read through (Bulk age until ready to bottle)

Muscadine Pyment "Semi-Sweet" Grape Mead

Yield: 1 gallon   OG: 1.106   FG: 1.015   ABV: 12%
Starting Brix: 25.17   Final Brix: 3.83

Primary

Yeast: 2 grams, Lalvin, K1V-1116
GoFerm: 2.50 grams
Nutrients: 1.89 grams Fermaid-O (0.47 grams each at 24, 48, 72 hours after pitching yeast. 4th dose to be administered at either the 1/3 sugar break or on 7th day)
Wildflower Honey: 1.68 lbs.
Grapes, Muscadine: 5.5 lbs. (frozen, thawed and semi-crushed)
Pectic Enzyme: per manufacturer's direction
Potassium Bicarbonate: ½ tsp. (to buffer the pH of the grapes a bit)

Secondary

Sodium Metabisuphite and Potassium Sorbate (per manufacturer's directions)
Let sit at cellar or room temperature until clear

Final Racking

Rack mead one final time and let it sit until the mead is clear enough to read through. (Bulk age until ready to bottle)

Directions:
- Before starting, clean and sanitize all of your equipment

Must Preparation
- Pour 1 quart of water into a large stock pot and bring to a low boil
- Remove from the heat and blend in the honey, stirring until it is completely dissolved
- Add juice from semi crushed fruit
- Add additional water to bring total liquid volume to 1 gallon
- Allow must to cool to room temperature then take a gravity reading
- Pour the cooled must into a 2 gallon brewing bucket and cover with a sanitary cloth and a large rubber band

Yeast Starter
- Mix GoFerm with 50 ml of hot water
- Allow mixture to cool to 104F then add your yeast and stir until dissolved
- Let this mixture sit for 15-20 minutes to allow it to activate and grow into a nice healthy colony

Primary
- When the temperature of the yeast starter drops to within 10 degrees of the must, pour it into the primary bucket and stir it thoroughly to disperse
- Add remainder of semi crushed fruit
- Add nutrients (Fermaid-O) as directed above
- Add Pectic Enzyme: per manufacturer's direction
- Aerate must twice daily until 1/3 sugar break then once daily until 2/3 sugar break
- When SG reaches target FG, rack to secondary

Secondary
- Rack primary must into a clean glass carboy over Sodium Metabisuphite and Potassium Sorbate to kill any remaining yeast and leave most of the sediment behind
- Add an airlock and leave in secondary until it clears

Final Racking
- Rack mead one final time and let it sit until the mead is clear enough to read through (Bulk age until ready to bottle)

White Pyment "Semi-Sweet" Grape Mead

Yield: 1 gallon   OG: 1.106   FG: 1.015   ABV: 12%
Starting Brix: 25.17   Final Brix: 3.83

Primary
Yeast: 2 grams, Red Star, Montrachet
GoFerm: 2.50 grams
Nutrients: 6 grams Fermaid-O (1.5 grams each at 24, 48, 72 hours after pitching yeast. 4th dose to be administered at either the 1/3 sugar break or on 7th day)
Wildflower Honey: 2.6 lbs.
Welch's 100% White Grape Juice: 2 cans
Pectic Enzyme: per manufacturer's direction

Secondary
Sodium Metabisuphite and Potassium Sorbate (per manufacturer's directions)
Let sit at cellar or room temperature until clear

Final Racking
Rack mead one final time and let it sit until the mead is clear enough to read through. (Bulk age until ready to bottle)

Directions:
- Before starting, clean and sanitize all of your equipment

Must Preparation
- Pour concentrated grape juice into a clean glass, or Pyrex, measuring cup.
- Pour 6 cans of water into a large stockpot and bring to a low boil.
- Remove from the heat and blend in the honey, stirring until it is completely dissolved
- Add the frozen juice and stir until thoroughly blended.
- Add additional water to bring total liquid volume to 1 gallon
- Allow must to cool to room temperature then take a gravity reading.
- Adjust gravity to Brix 25.17 by adding more honey or water as needed.
- Pour the cooled must into a 2 gallon brewing bucket and cover with a sanitary cloth and a large rubber band

Yeast Starter
- Mix 2.5 grams GoFerm with 50 ml of boiling water and 2 grams of sugar.
- Allow mixture to cool to 104F then add your yeast and stir until well dispersed.
- Let this mixture sit for 15-20 minutes to allow it to activate and grow into a nice healthy colony

Primary
- When the temperature of the yeast starter drops to within 10 degrees of the must, pour it into the primary bucket and stir it thoroughly to disperse.
- Add nutrients (Fermaid-O) as directed above.
- Add Pectic Enzyme: per manufacturer's direction
- Aerate must twice daily until 1/3 sugar break then once daily until 2/3 sugar break.
- When OG reaches target FG, rack to secondary.

Secondary
- Rack primary must into a clean glass carboy over Sodium Metabisuphite and Potassium Sorbate to kill any remaining yeast and leave most of the sediment behind
- Add an airlock
- Leave in secondary until it clears

Final Racking
- Rack mead one final time and let it sit until the mead is clear enough to read through (Bulk age until ready to bottle)

M2C – Berry Meads

Berry melomels provide a wonderful blend of honey and fruity notes that combine to produce an extremely enjoyable beverage. They tend to be pretty straight forward in what they offer, but finding the perfect balance between honey and berry flavors, and just the right mix of berries, will provide the mead maker with an endless variety of options to try and pursue until they get it "just right".

Black Currant (Black Mead)

Yield: 1 gallon   OG: 1.132   FG: 1.025   ABV: 14%
Starting Brix: 30.53   Final Brix: 6.33

Primary
Yeast: 2 grams, Lalvin 71B-1122
GoFerm: 2.50 grams
Nutrients: 2.29 grams Fermaid-O (0.57 grams each at 24, 48, 72, & 96 hours after pitching yeast.)
Pectic Enzyme: per manufacturer's direction
Blackberry Honey: 3.53 lbs.
Black Currants: 2.5 lbs. (frozen, thawed, & semi-crushed)

Secondary
Sodium Metabisuphite and Potassium Sorbate (per manufacturer's direction)
Let sit at cellar or room temperature until clear

Final Racking
Rack mead one final time and let it sit until the mead is clear enough to read through. (Bulk age until ready to bottle)

Directions:
- Before starting, clean and sanitize all of your equipment

Must Preparation
- Pour 2 quarts of water into a large stock pot and bring to a low boil
- Remove from the heat and blend in the honey, stirring until it is completely dissolved
- Add additional water to bring total volume to 1 gallon
- Allow must to cool to room temperature then take a gravity reading
- Pour the cooled must into a 2 gallon brewing bucket and cover with a sanitary cloth and a large rubber band

Yeast Starter
- Mix GoFerm with 50 ml of hot water
- Allow mixture to cool to 104F then add your yeast and stir until dissolved
- Let this mixture sit for 15-20 minutes to allow it to activate and grow into a nice healthy colony

Primary
- When the temperature of the yeast starter drops to within 10 degrees of the must, pour it into the primary bucket and stir it thoroughly to disperse
- Add Black Currants
- Add nutrients (Fermaid-O) as directed above
- Add Pectic Enzyme: per manufacturer's direction
- Aerate must twice daily until 1/3 sugar break then once daily until 2/3 sugar break

Secondary
- On day five (5), strain must (through a sieve) into a clean glass carboy to remove the skins
- Add an airlock
- When Target gravity is reached, add Sodium Metabisuphite and Potassium Sorbate to kill any remaining yeast
- Leave in secondary until it clears

Final Racking
- Rack mead one final time then bulk age until ready to bottle

Blackberry Blast "Sweet" Melomel

Yield: 1 gallon   OG: 1.132   FG: 1.025   ABV: 14%

Starting Brix: 30.53   Final Brix: 6.33

Primary
Yeast: 2 grams, Lalvin, K1V-1116

GoFerm: 2.50 grams

Nutrients: 5.50 grams Fermaid-O (1.37 grams each at 24, 48, 72 hours after pitching yeast. 4th dose to be administered at either the 1/3 sugar break or on 7th day)

Cranberry Honey: 3.82 lbs.

Secondary
Sodium Metabisuphite and Potassium Sorbate (per manufacturer's direction)

Blackberries: 2 lbs. (frozen, thawed, & semi crushed)

Pectic Enzyme: per manufacturer's direction

Let sit at cellar or room temperature until fruit loses its color (turns white)

Final Racking
Rack mead one final time and let it sit until the mead is clear enough to read through. (Bulk age until ready to bottle)

"LET THERE BE MELOMELS!" BY ROBERT RATLIFF

Directions:
- Before starting, clean and sanitize all of your equipment

Must Preparation
- Pour 2 quarts of water into a large stock pot and bring to a low boil
- Remove from the heat and blend in the honey, stirring until completely dissolved
- Add additional water to bring total volume to 1 gallon
- Allow must to cool to room temperature then take a gravity reading
- Pour the cooled must into a 2 gallon brewing bucket and cover with a sanitary cloth and a large rubber band

Yeast Starter
- Mix GoFerm with 50 ml of hot water
- Allow mixture to cool to 104F then add your yeast and stir until dissolved
- Let this mixture sit for 15-20 minutes to allow it to activate

Primary
- When the temperature of the yeast starter drops to within 10 degrees of the must, pour it into the primary bucket and stir it thoroughly to disperse
- Add nutrients (Fermaid-O) as directed above
- Aerate must twice daily until 1/3 sugar break then once daily until 2/3 sugar break
- When SG reaches target FG, rack to secondary

Secondary
- Rack primary must into a clean glass carboy over Sodium Metabisuphite and Potassium Sorbate to kill any remaining yeast and leave most of the sediment behind
- Add Blackberries (frozen, thawed, & semi crushed)
- Add Pectic Enzyme: per manufacturer's direction
- Add an airlock
- Leave in secondary until fruit loses its color (turns white)

Final Racking
- Rack mead one final time and let it sit until the mead is clear enough to read through (Bulk age until ready to bottle)

Blueberry Bliss "Semi-Sweet" Melomel

Yield: 1 gallon   OG: 1.106   FG: 1.015   ABV: 12%
Starting Brix: 25.17   Final Brix: 3.83

Primary
Yeast: 2 grams, Lalvin, 71B-1122
GoFerm: 2.50 grams
Nutrients: 1.89 grams Fermaid-O (0.47 grams each at 24, 48, 72 hours after pitching yeast. 4th dose to be administered at either the 1/3 sugar break or on 7th day)
Blueberry Honey: 2.96 lbs.
Blueberries: 1.0 lb. (frozen, thawed, & semi crushed)
Pectic Enzyme: per manufacturer's direction

Secondary
Sodium Metabisuphite and Potassium Sorbate (per manufacturer's direction)
Let sit at cellar or room temperature until clear
Blueberries: 1.0 lb. (frozen, thawed, & semi crushed)
Lemon: ½ lemon (juice and zest)

Final Racking
Rack mead one final time and let it sit until the mead is clear enough to read through. (Bulk age until ready to bottle)

Directions:
- Before starting, clean and sanitize all of your equipment

Must Preparation
- Pour 2 quarts of water into a large stock pot and bring to a low boil
- Remove from the heat and blend in the honey, stirring until it is completely dissolved
- Add additional water to bring total volume to 1 gallon
- Allow must to cool to room temperature then take a gravity reading
- Pour the cooled must into a 2 gallon brewing bucket and cover with a sanitary cloth and a large rubber band

Yeast Starter
- Mix GoFerm with 50 ml of hot water
- Allow mixture to cool to 104F then add your yeast and stir until dissolved
- Let this mixture sit for 15-20 minutes to allow it to activate and grow into a nice healthy colony

Primary
- When the temperature of the yeast starter drops to within 10 degrees of the must, pour it into the primary bucket and stir it thoroughly to disperse
- Add 1 lb. blueberries
- Add nutrients (Fermaid-O) as directed above
- Add Pectic Enzyme: per manufacturer's direction
- Aerate must twice daily until 1/3 sugar break then once daily until 2/3 sugar break
- When SG reaches target FG, rack to secondary

Secondary
- Rack primary must into a clean glass carboy over Sodium Metabisuphite and Potassium Sorbate to kill any remaining yeast and leave most of the sediment behind
- Add remaining blueberries, lemon juice, & zest
- Add an airlock and leave in secondary until fruit loses its color (turns white)

Final Racking
- Rack mead one final time and let it sit until the mead is clear enough to read through (Bulk age until ready to bottle)

Cranberry "Semi-Sweet" Mead

Yield: 1 gallon   OG: 1.106   FG: 1.015   ABV: 12%
Starting Brix: 25.17   Final Brix: 3.83

Primary

Yeast: 2 grams, Lalvin, 71B-1122
GoFerm: 2.50 grams
Nutrients: 4.53 grams Fermaid-O (1.13 grams each at 24, 48, 72 hours after pitching yeast. 4th dose to be administered at either the 1/3 sugar break or on 7th day)
Cranberry Honey: 3.01 lbs.
Cranberries: 1.5 lbs.
Pectic Enzyme: per manufacturer's direction

Secondary

Sodium Metabisuphite and Potassium Sorbate (per manufacturer's direction)
Let sit at cellar or room temperature until clear

Final Racking

Rack mead one final time and let it sit until the mead is clear enough to read through. (Bulk age until ready to bottle)

"LET THERE BE MELOMELS!" BY ROBERT RATLIFF

Directions:
- Before starting, clean and sanitize all of your equipment

Must Preparation
- Pour 2 quarts of water into a large stock pot and bring to a low boil
- Add cranberries and stir until they are fully blanched
- Remove from the heat and blend in the honey, stirring until it is completely dissolved
- Add additional water to bring total volume to 1 gallon
- Allow must to cool to room temperature then take a gravity reading
- Pour the cooled must into a 2 gallon brewing bucket and cover with a sanitary cloth and a large rubber band

Yeast Starter
- Mix GoFerm with 50 ml of hot water
- Allow mixture to cool to 104F then add your yeast and stir until dissolved
- Let this mixture sit for 15-20 minutes to allow it to activate and grow into a nice healthy colony

Primary
- When the temperature of the yeast starter drops to within 10 degrees of the must, pour it into the primary bucket and stir it thoroughly to disperse
- Add nutrients (Fermaid-O) as directed above
- Add Pectic Enzyme: per manufacturer's direction
- Aerate must twice daily until 1/3 sugar break then once daily until 2/3 sugar break
- When SG reaches target FG, add Sodium Metabisuphite and Potassium Sorbate to stabilize the must and stop fermentation
- Set aside until fruit loses its color (1 month or until fruit turns white)
- Rack to secondary

Secondary
- Rack primary must into a clean glass carboy leaving the fruit and sediment behind
- Add and airlock and leave in secondary until it clears

Final Racking
- Rack mead one final time and let it sit until the mead is clear enough to read through (Bulk age until ready to bottle)

Raspberry "Sweet" Melomel

Yield: 1 gallon   OG: 1.132   FG: 1.025   ABV: 14%

Starting Brix: 30.53   Final Brix: 6.33

Primary

Yeast: 2 grams, Lalvin, K1V-1116

GoFerm: 2.50 grams

Nutrients: 5.50 grams Fermaid-O (1.37 grams each at 24, 48, 72 hours after pitching yeast. 4th dose to be administered at either the 1/3 sugar break or on 7th day)

Cranberry Honey: 3.82 lbs.

Secondary

Sodium Metabisuphite and Potassium Sorbate (per manufacturer's direction)

Raspberries: 1.0 lb. (frozen, thawed, & semi crushed)

Pectic Enzyme: Per manufacturer's directions

Let sit at cellar or room temperature until fruit loses it's color (turns white)

Final Racking

Rack mead one final time and let it sit until the mead is clear enough to read through. (Bulk age until ready to bottle)

"LET THERE BE MELOMELS!" BY ROBERT RATLIFF

Directions:
- Before starting, clean and sanitize all of your equipment

Must Preparation
- Pour 2 quarts of water into a large stock pot and bring to a low boil
- Remove from the heat and blend in the honey, stirring until it is completely dissolved
- Add additional water to bring total volume to 1 gallon
- Allow must to cool to room temperature then take a gravity reading
- Pour the cooled must into a 2 gallon brewing bucket and cover with a sanitary cloth and a large rubber band

Yeast Starter
- Mix GoFerm with 50 ml of hot water
- Allow mixture to cool to 104F then add your yeast and stir until dissolved
- Let this mixture sit for 15-20 minutes to allow it to activate and grow into a nice healthy colony

Primary
- When the temperature of the yeast starter drops to within 10 degrees of the must, pour it into the primary bucket and stir it thoroughly to disperse
- Add nutrients (Fermaid-O) as directed above
- Aerate must twice daily until 1/3 sugar break then once daily until 2/3 sugar break
- When OG reaches target FG, rack to secondary

Secondary
- Rack primary must into a clean glass carboy over Sodium Metabisuphite and Potassium Sorbate to kill any remaining yeast and leave most of the sediment behind
- Add Raspberries (frozen, thawed, & semi crushed)
- Add Pectic Enzyme: per manufacturer's direction
- Add an airlock
- Leave in secondary until fruit loses it's color (turns white)

Final Racking
- Rack mead one final time and let it sit until the mead is clear enough to read through (Bulk age until ready to bottle)

Strawberry "Semi-Sweet" Melomel

Yield: 1 gallon   OG: 1.106   FG: 1.015   ABV: 12%

Starting Brix: 25.17   Final Brix: 3.83

Primary

Yeast: 2 grams, Lalvin, 71B-1122

GoFerm: 2.50 grams

Nutrients: 1.89 grams Fermaid-O (0.47 grams each at 24, 48, 72 hours after pitching yeast. 4th dose to be administered at either the 1/3 sugar break or on 7th day)

Strawberries: 1.5 lbs. (frozen, thawed, & semi crushed)

Pectic Enzyme: Per manufacturer's directions

Wildflower Honey: 2.97 lbs.

Secondary

Sodium Metabisuphite and Potassium Sorbate (per manufacturer's direction)

Acid Blend: 5 grams

Strawberries: 1.5 lbs. (frozen, thawed, & semi crushed)

Set aside in a cool dark place until clear

Final Racking

Rack mead one final time and let it sit until the mead is clear enough to read through. (Bulk age until ready to bottle)

Directions:
- Before starting, clean and sanitize all of your equipment

Must Preparation
- Pour 2 quarts of water into a large stock pot and bring to a low boil
- Remove from the heat and blend in the honey, stirring until it is completely dissolved
- Add additional water to bring total volume to 1 gallon
- Allow must to cool to room temperature then take a gravity reading
- Pour the cooled must into a 2 gallon brewing bucket and cover with a sanitary cloth and a large rubber band

Yeast Starter
- Mix GoFerm with 50 ml of hot water
- Allow mixture to cool to 104F then add your yeast and stir until dissolved
- Let this mixture sit for 15-20 minutes to allow it to activate and grow into a nice healthy colony

Primary
- When the temperature of the yeast starter drops to within 10 degrees of the must, pour it into the primary bucket and stir it thoroughly to disperse
- Add strawberries (frozen, thawed, & semi-crushed)
- Add nutrients (Fermaid-O) as directed above
- Add Pectic Enzyme: Per manufacturer's directions
- Aerate must twice daily until 1/3 sugar break then once daily until 2/3 sugar break
- When OG reaches target FG, rack to secondary

Secondary
- Rack primary must into a clean glass carboy over Sodium Metabisuphite and Potassium Sorbate to kill any remaining yeast and leave most of the sediment behind
- Add remaining strawberries
- Add Acid Blend
- Add an airlock
- Leave in secondary until fruit loses its color (turns white)

Final Racking
- Rack mead one final time and let it sit until the mead is clear enough to read through (Bulk age until ready to bottle)

M2D – Stone Fruit Meads

Stone fruit Meads are simply Melomels that use a type of fruit (or fruits) that has a stone-like pit rather than a normal seed. Cherries, Plums, Peaches, Apricots, etc. are examples of "Stone Fruits".

Some people ferment with the entire fruit, and some don't. Contrary to popular belief, you can't 'poison yourself' (or others) by letting a pit or two stay in your mead, it takes a LOT of pits (like quarts) to make up enough of what is in the pits to make you sick. So don't worry about it.

Cherry Melomel (Sour)

Yield: 1 gallon   OG: 1.106   FG: 1.015   ABV: 12%
Starting Brix: 25.17   Final Brix: 3.83

Primary

Yeast: 2 grams, Lalvin, 71B-1122
GoFerm: 2.50 grams
Nutrients: 1.89 grams Fermaid-O (0.47 grams each at 24, 48, 72 hours after pitching yeast. 4th dose to be administered at either the 1/3 sugar break or on 7th day)
Cranberry Honey: 2.7 lbs.
Sour Cherries: 4 lbs. (pitted, frozen, thawed, & semi crushed)
Pectic Enzyme: per manufacturer's direction

Secondary

Sodium Metabisuphite and Potassium Sorbate (per manufacturer's direction)
Acid Blend: 1/3 tsp.
Let sit at cellar or room temperature until clear

Final Racking

Rack mead one final time and let it sit until the mead is clear enough to read through. (Bulk age until ready to bottle)

Directions:

- Before starting, clean and sanitize all of your equipment

Must Preparation

- Pour 2 quarts of water into a large stock pot and bring to a low boil
- Remove from the heat and blend in the honey, stirring until it is completely dissolved
- Add additional water to bring total volume to 1 gallon
- Allow must to cool to room temperature then take a gravity reading
- Pour the cooled must into a 2 gallon brewing bucket and cover with a sanitary cloth and a large rubber band

Yeast Starter

- Mix GoFerm with 50 ml of hot water
- Allow mixture to cool to 104F then add your yeast and stir until dissolved
- Let this mixture sit for 15-20 minutes to allow it to activate and grow into a nice healthy colony

Primary

- When the temperature of the yeast starter drops to within 10 degrees of the must, pour it into the primary bucket and stir it thoroughly to disperse
- Add crushed cherries
- Add nutrients (Fermaid-O) as directed above
- Add Pectic Enzyme: per manufacturer's direction
- Aerate must twice daily until 1/3 sugar break then once daily until 2/3 sugar break
- When SG reaches target FG, rack to secondary

Secondary

- Rack primary must into a clean glass carboy over Sodium Metabisuphite and Potassium Sorbate to kill any remaining yeast and leave most of the sediment behind
- Add Acid Blend
- Add an airlock and leave in secondary until it clears

Final Racking

- Rack mead one final time and let it sit until the mead is clear enough to read through (Bulk age until ready to bottle)

Mango Melomel "Semi-Sweet"

Yield: 1 gallon OG: 1.106 FG: 1.015 ABV: 12%
Starting Brix: 25.17 Final Brix: 3.83

Primary
Yeast: 2 grams, Lalvin, ICV-D47
GoFerm: 2.50 grams
Nutrients: 1.89 grams Fermaid-O (0.47 grams each at 24, 48, 72 hours after pitching yeast. 4th dose to be administered at either the 1/3 sugar break or on 7th day)
Orange Blossom Honey: 2.91 lbs.
Mango: 1 lb. (chucked, frozen, thawed, & slightly crushed)
Pectic Enzyme: per manufacturer's direction

Secondary
Sodium Metabisuphite and Potassium Sorbate (per manufacturer's direction)
Let sit at cellar or room temperature until clear

Final Racking
Rack mead one final time and let it sit until the mead is clear enough to read through. (Bulk age until ready to bottle)

Directions:
- Before starting, clean and sanitize all of your equipment

Must Preparation
- Pour 2 quarts of water into a large stock pot and bring to a low boil
- Remove from the heat and blend in the honey, stirring until it is completely dissolved
- Add additional water to bring total volume to 1 gallon
- Allow must to cool to room temperature then take a gravity reading
- Pour the cooled must into a 2 gallon brewing bucket and cover with a sanitary cloth and a large rubber band

Yeast Starter
- Mix GoFerm with 50 ml of hot water
- Allow mixture to cool to 104F then add your yeast and stir until dissolved
- Let this mixture sit for 15-20 minutes to allow it to activate and grow into a nice healthy colony

Primary
- When the temperature of the yeast starter drops to within 10 degrees of the must, pour it into the primary bucket and stir it thoroughly to disperse
- Add the mango chunks
- Add Pectic Enzyme: per manufacturer's direction
- Add nutrients (Fermaid-O) as directed above
- Aerate must twice daily until 1/3 sugar break then once daily until 2/3 sugar break
- When SG reaches target FG, rack to secondary

Secondary
- Rack primary must into a clean glass carboy over Sodium Metabisuphite and Potassium Sorbate to kill any remaining yeast and leave most of the sediment behind
- Add an airlock and leave in secondary until it clears

Final Racking
- Rack mead one final time and let it sit until the mead is clear enough to read through (Bulk age until ready to bottle)

M2E – Other/Mixed Fruit Meads

This category covers any melomels using a blend of 2 or more types of fruit. Multiple fruit additions add great complexity to the mead and can combine to create truly unique combinations of flavor to be experienced by the recipient. Some fruits combine quite naturally while others can create quite a surprise for the adventurous mead drinker

Apple-Blackberry "Sweet" Cyser

Yield: 1 gallon   OG: 1.117   FG: 1.025   ABV: 14%

Starting Brix: 27.37   Final Brix: 6.33

Primary

Unfiltered Apple Juice: 1 gallon

Yeast: 1 gram, Lalvin, D-47

GoFerm: 2.50 grams

Nutrients: 4.11 grams Fermaid-O (1.03 grams each at 24, 48, 72 hours after pitching yeast. 4th dose to be administered at either the 1/3 sugar break or on 7th day)

Pectic Enzyme: per manufacturer's direction

Blackberry Honey: 2.05 lbs.

Secondary

Blackberries: 0.75 lbs. (frozen, thawed, and semi-crushed)

Sodium Metabisuphite and Potassium Sorbate (per manufacturer's direction)

Final Racking

Rack mead one final time and let it sit until the mead is clear enough to read through. (Bulk age until ready to bottle)

Directions:
- Before starting, clean and sanitize all of your equipment.

Must Preparation
- Pour 2 quarts of apple juice into a large stock pot and bring to a low boil
- Remove from the heat and blend in the honey, stirring until it is completely dissolved
- Add additional juice to bring total volume to 1 gallon
- Allow must to cool to room temperature then take a gravity reading
- Pour the cooled must into a 2 gallon brewing bucket and cover with a sanitary cloth and a large rubber band

Yeast Starter
- Mix GoFerm with 50 ml of hot water
- Allow mixture to cool to 104F then add your yeast and stir until dissolved
- Let this mixture sit for 15-20 minutes to allow it to activate and grow into a nice healthy colony

Primary
- When the temperature of the yeast starter drops to within 10 degrees of the must, pour it into the primary bucket and stir it thoroughly to disperse
- Add nutrients (Fermaid-O) as directed above
- Add Pectic Enzyme: per manufacturer's direction
- Aerate must twice daily until 1/3 sugar break then once daily until 2/3 sugar break
- When SG reaches target FG, rack to secondary

Secondary
- Rack primary must into a clean glass carboy over Sodium Metabisuphite and Potassium Sorbate to kill any remaining yeast and leave most of the sediment behind
- Add fruit
- Add an airlock
- Leave in secondary until it clears and fruit loses its color (turns white)

Final Racking
- Rack mead one final time and let it sit until the mead is clear enough to read through (Bulk age until ready to bottle)

Apple-Blueberry-Cranberry "Semi-Sweet" Cyser

Yield: 1 gallon   OG: 1.106   FG: 1.015   ABV: 12%
Starting Brix: 25.17   Final Brix: 3.83

Primary

Yeast: 2 grams, Lalvin, ICV-D47

GoFerm: 2.50 grams

Nutrients: 1.89 grams Fermaid-O (0.47 grams each at 24, 48, 72 hours after pitching yeast. 4th dose to be administered at either the 1/3 sugar break or on 7th day)

Wildflower Honey: 1.60 lbs.

Cranberries: 1 lb.

Blueberries: 1 lb.

Pectic Enzyme: per manufacturer's direction

Secondary

Sodium Metabisuphite and Potassium Sorbate (per manufacturer's direction)

Let sit at cellar or room temperature until clear

Final Racking

Rack mead one final time and let it sit until the mead is clear enough to read through. (Bulk age until ready to bottle)

Directions:
- Before starting, clean and sanitize all of your equipment

Must Preparation
- Pour 2 quarts of apple juice into a large stock pot and bring to a low boil
- Add cranberries and stir slowly until they have blanched
- Remove from the heat and blend in the honey, stirring until it is completely dissolved
- Add additional juice to bring total volume to 1 gallon
- Allow must to cool to room temperature then take a gravity reading
- Pour the cooled must into a 2 gallon brewing bucket and cover with a sanitary cloth and a large rubber band

Yeast Starter
- Mix GoFerm with 50 ml of hot water
- Allow mixture to cool to 104F then add your yeast and stir until dissolved
- Let this mixture sit for 15-20 minutes to allow it to activate

Primary
- When the temperature of the yeast starter drops to within 10 degrees of the must, pour it into the primary bucket and stir it thoroughly to disperse
- Add blueberries (frozen, thawed, and semi-crushed)
- Add Pectic Enzyme: per manufacturer's direction
- Add nutrients (Fermaid-O) as directed above
- Aerate must twice daily until 1/3 sugar break then once daily until 2/3 sugar break
- When SG reaches target FG, add Sodium Metabisuphite and Potassium Sorbate to stabilize fermentation
- Leave in primary until fruit loses its color (turns white)

Secondary
- Rack primary must into a clean glass carboy leaving the fruit and most of the sediment behind
- Add an airlock and leave in secondary until the mead clears

Final Racking
- Rack mead one final time and let it sit until the mead is clear enough to read through (Bulk age until ready to bottle)

Apple-Blueberry "Semi-Sweet" Cyser

Yield: 1 gallon   OG: 1.091   FG: 1.015   ABV: 12%
Starting Brix: 21.89   Final Brix: 3.83

Primary

Unfiltered Apple Juice: 1 gallon
Yeast: 1 gram, Lalvin, D-47
GoFerm: 1.25 grams
Blueberries: 0.75 lbs. (frozen, thawed, and semi-crushed)
Nutrients: 1.64 grams Fermaid-O (0.41 grams each at 24, 48, 72 hours after pitching
yeast. 4th dose to be administered at either the 1/3 sugar break or on 7th day)
Pectic Enzyme: per manufacturer's direction
Cranberry Honey: 1.26 lbs.
Sodium Metabisuphite and Potassium Sorbate (per manufacturer's direction)

Secondary

Set aside in a cool place until mead clears

Final Racking

Rack mead one final time and let it sit until the mead is clear enough to read
through. (Bulk age until ready to bottle)

Directions:
- Before starting, clean and sanitize all of your equipment.

Must Preparation
- Pour 2 quarts of apple juice into a large stock pot and bring to a low boil
- Remove from the heat and blend in the honey, stirring until it is completely dissolved
- Add additional juice to bring total volume to 1 gallon
- Allow must to cool to room temperature then take a gravity reading
- Pour the cooled must into a 2 gallon brewing bucket and cover with a sanitary cloth and a large rubber band

Yeast Starter
- Mix GoFerm with 25 ml of hot water
- Allow mixture to cool to 104F then add your yeast and stir until dissolved
- Let this mixture sit for 15-20 minutes to allow it to activate and grow into a nice healthy colony

Primary
- When the temperature of the yeast starter drops to within 10 degrees of the must, pour it into the primary bucket and stir it thoroughly to disperse
- Add fruit
- Add nutrients (Fermaid-O) as directed above
- Add Pectic Enzyme: per manufacturer's direction
- Aerate must twice daily until 1/3 sugar break then once daily until 2/3 sugar break
- When SG reaches target FG, add Sodium Metabisuphite and Potassium Sorbate to kill any remaining yeast and stabilize the mead
- Set aside until mead clears and fruit loses its color (turns white) the rack to secondary

Secondary
- Rack mead into a clean glass carboy leaving the fruit and sediment behind
- Add an airlock
- Leave in secondary until it clears completely

Final Racking
- Rack mead one final time and let it sit until the mead is clear enough to read through (Bulk age until ready to bottle)

Apple-Cranberry "Sweet" Cyser

Yield: 1 gallon   OG: 1.117   FG: 1.025   ABV: 14%
Starting Brix: 27.37   Final Brix: 6.33

Primary
Yeast: 2 grams, Lalvin, D-47
GoFerm: 2.50 grams
Nutrients: 2.05 grams Fermaid-O (0.51 grams each at 24, 48, 72 hours after pitching yeast. 4th dose to be administered at either the 1/3 sugar break or on 7th day)
Apple Juice: 1 gallon, unfiltered
Cranberry Honey: 1.96 lbs.
Cranberries: 1.5 lbs.
Pectic Enzyme: per manufacturer's direction

Secondary
Sodium Metabisuphite and Potassium Sorbate (per manufacturer's direction)
Let sit at cellar or room temperature until clear

Final Racking
Rack mead one final time and let it sit until the mead is clear enough to read through. (Bulk age until ready to bottle)

Directions:
- Before starting, clean and sanitize all of your equipment

Must Preparation
- Pour 2 quarts of apple juice into a large stock pot and bring to a low boil
- Add cranberries and stir until they are fully blanched
- Remove from the heat and blend in the honey, stirring until it is completely dissolved
- Add additional juice to bring total volume to 1 gallon (take into account for fruit displacement)
- Allow must to cool to room temperature then take a gravity reading
- Pour the cooled must into a 2 gallon brewing bucket and cover with a sanitary cloth and a large rubber band

Yeast Starter
- Mix GoFerm with 50 ml of hot water
- Allow mixture to cool to 104F then add your yeast and stir until dissolved
- Let this mixture sit for 15-20 minutes to allow it to activate and grow into a nice healthy colony

Primary
- When the temperature of the yeast starter drops to within 10 degrees of the must, pour it into the primary bucket and stir it thoroughly to disperse
- Add Pectic Enzyme: per manufacturer's direction
- Add nutrients (Fermaid-O) as directed above
- Aerate must twice daily until 1/3 sugar break then once daily until 2/3 sugar break
- When SG reaches target FG, add Sodium Metabisuphite and Potassium Sorbate to stabilize the must and stop fermentation
- Set aside until fruit loses its color (1 month or until fruit turns white)
- Rack to secondary

Secondary
- Rack primary must into a clean glass carboy leaving the fruit and sediment behind
- Add an airlock and leave in secondary until it clears

Final Racking
- Rack mead one final time and bulk age until ready to bottle

Apple-Raspberry "Sweet" Cyser

Yield: 1 gallon   OG: 1.117   FG: 1.025   ABV: 14%
Starting Brix: 27.37   Final Brix: 6.33

Primary

Unfiltered Apple Juice: 1 gallon
Yeast: 1 gram, Lalvin, D-47
GoFerm: 2.50 grams
Nutrients: 4.11 grams Fermaid-O (1.03 grams each at 24, 48, 72 hours after pitching yeast. 4th dose to be administered at either the 1/3 sugar break or on 7th day)
Pectic Enzyme: per manufacturer's direction
Wildflower Honey: 2.05 lbs.

Secondary

Raspberries: 0.50 lbs. (frozen, thawed, and semi-crushed)
Sodium Metabisuphite and Potassium Sorbate (per manufacturer's direction)

Final Racking

Rack mead one final time and let it sit until the mead is clear enough to read through. (Bulk age until ready to bottle)

Directions:
- Before starting, clean and sanitize all of your equipment.

Must Preparation
- Pour 2 quarts of apple juice into a large stock pot and bring to a low boil
- Remove from the heat and blend in the honey, stirring until it is completely dissolved
- Add additional juice to bring total volume to 1 gallon
- Allow must to cool to room temperature then take a gravity reading
- Pour the cooled must into a 2 gallon brewing bucket and cover with a sanitary cloth and a large rubber band

Yeast Starter
- Mix GoFerm with 50 ml of hot water
- Allow mixture to cool to 104F then add your yeast and stir until dissolved
- Let this mixture sit for 15-20 minutes to allow it to activate and grow into a nice healthy colony

Primary
- When the temperature of the yeast starter drops to within 10 degrees of the must, pour it into the primary bucket and stir it thoroughly to disperse
- Add fruit
- Add nutrients (Fermaid-O) as directed above
- Add Pectic Enzyme: per manufacturer's direction
- Aerate must twice daily until 1/3 sugar break then once daily until 2/3 sugar break
- When SG reaches target FG, rack to secondary

Secondary
- Rack primary must into a clean glass carboy over Sodium Metabisuphite and Potassium Sorbate to kill any remaining yeast and leave most of the sediment behind
- Add fruit
- Add an airlock
- Leave in secondary until it clears and fruit loses its color (turns white)

Final Racking
- Rack mead one final time and let it sit until the mead is clear enough to read through (Bulk age until ready to bottle)

Apple-Sour Cherry "Semi-Sweet" Cyser

Yield: 1 gallon   OG: 1.091   FG: 1.015   ABV: 12%
Starting Brix: 21.89   Final Brix: 3.83

Primary

Unfiltered Apple Juice: 1 gallon
Yeast: 1 gram, Lalvin, D-47
GoFerm: 1.25 grams
Sour Cherries: 1.5 lbs. (frozen, thawed, and semi-crushed)
Nutrients: 1.64 grams Fermaid-O (0.41 grams each at 24, 48, 72 hours after pitching yeast. 4th dose to be administered at either the 1/3 sugar break or on 7th day)
Pectic Enzyme: per manufacturer's direction
Wildflower Honey: 1.18 lbs.

Secondary

Sodium Metabisuphite and Potassium Sorbate (per manufacturer's direction)

Final Racking

Rack mead one final time and let it sit until the mead is clear enough to read through. (Bulk age until ready to bottle)

Directions:
- Before starting, clean and sanitize all of your equipment.

Must Preparation
- Pour 2 quarts of apple juice into a large stock pot and bring to a low boil
- Remove from the heat and blend in the honey, stirring until it is completely dissolved
- Add additional juice to bring total volume to 1 gallon
- Allow must to cool to room temperature then take a gravity reading
- Pour the cooled must into a 2 gallon brewing bucket and cover with a sanitary cloth and a large rubber band

Yeast Starter
- Mix GoFerm with 25 ml of hot water
- Allow mixture to cool to 104F then add your yeast and stir until dissolved
- Let this mixture sit for 15-20 minutes to allow it to activate and grow into a nice healthy colony

Primary
- When the temperature of the yeast starter drops to within 10 degrees of the must, pour it into the primary bucket and stir it thoroughly to disperse
- Add fruit
- Add nutrients (Fermaid-O) as directed above
- Add Pectic Enzyme: per manufacturer's direction
- Aerate must twice daily until 1/3 sugar break then once daily until 2/3 sugar break
- When SG reaches target FG, add Sodium Metabisuphite and Potassium Sorbate to kill any remaining yeast and stabilize the mead
- Set aside until mead clears and fruit loses its color (turns white) the rack to secondary

Secondary
- Rack mead into a clean glass carboy leaving the fruit and sediment behind
- Add an airlock.
- Leave in secondary until it clears

Final Racking
- Rack mead one final time and let it sit until the mead is clear enough to read through (Bulk age until ready to bottle)

Black Currant-Blueberry-Blackberry

Yield: 1 gallon   OG: 1.106   FG: 1.015   ABV: 12%
Starting Brix: 25.17   Final Brix: 3.83

Primary
Yeast: 2 grams, Lalvin, 71B-1122
GoFerm: 2.50 grams
Nutrients: 1.89 grams Fermaid-O (0.47 grams each at 24, 48, 72 hours after pitching yeast. 4th dose to be administered at either the 1/3 sugar break or on 7th day)
Cranberry Honey: 2.94 lbs.
Pectic Enzyme: Per manufacturer's direction
Black Currants: 1 lb. (frozen, thawed, and semi-crushed)
Blueberries: 0.5 lbs. (frozen, thawed, and semi-crushed)

Secondary
Blackberries: 0.25 lbs. (frozen, thawed, and semi-crushed)
Sodium Metabisuphite and Potassium Sorbate (per manufacturer's direction)
Let sit at cellar or room temperature until fruit loses its color (turns white)

Final Racking
Rack mead one final time and let it sit until the mead is clear enough to read through. (Bulk age until ready to bottle)

"LET THERE BE MELOMELS!" BY ROBERT RATLIFF

Directions:
- Before starting, clean and sanitize all of your equipment

Must Preparation
- Pour 2 quarts of water into a large stock pot and bring to a low boil
- Remove from the heat and blend in the honey, stirring until it is completely dissolved
- Add additional water to bring total volume to 1 gallon
- Allow must to cool to room temperature then take a gravity reading
- Pour the cooled must into a 2 gallon brewing bucket and cover with a sanitary cloth and a large rubber band

Yeast Starter
- Mix GoFerm with 50 ml of hot water
- Allow mixture to cool to 104F then add your yeast and stir until dissolved
- Let this mixture sit for 15-20 minutes to allow it to activate and grow into a nice healthy colony

Primary
- When the temperature of the yeast starter drops to within 10 degrees of the must, pour it into the primary bucket and stir it thoroughly to disperse
- Add Black Currants and Blueberries
- Add nutrients (Fermaid-O) as directed above
- Add Pectic Enzyme: per manufacturer's direction
- Aerate must twice daily until 1/3 sugar break then once daily until 2/3 sugar break
- When SG reaches target FG, add Sodium Metabisuphite and Potassium Sorbate to kill any remaining yeast and stabilize the must
- Set aside in a cool place until mead clears and fruit loses its color (turns white)
- Rack to secondary

Secondary
- Rack primary must into a clean glass carboy leaving the spent fruit most of the sediment behind
- Add blackberries
- Add an airlock
- Leave in secondary until fruit loses its color (turns white)

Final Racking
- Rack mead one final time and let it sit until the mead is clear enough to read through (Bulk age until ready to bottle)

Blackberry-Blueberry-Raspberry-Sour Cherry Mead

Yield: 1 gallon   OG: 1.106   FG: 1.015   ABV: 12%
Starting Brix: 25.17   Final Brix: 3.83

Primary
Yeast: 2 grams, Lalvin, 71B-1122
GoFerm: 2.50 grams
Nutrients: 1.89 grams Fermaid-O (0.47 grams each at 24, 48, 72 hours after pitching yeast. 4th dose to be administered at either the 1/3 sugar break or on 7th day)
Pectic Enzyme: per manufacturer's direction
Blueberries: 0.5 lbs. (frozen, thawed, and semi-crushed)
Sour Cherries: 0.75 lbs. (frozen, thawed, and semi-crushed)
Wildflower Honey: 2.98 lbs.

Secondary
Sodium Metabisuphite and Potassium Sorbate (per manufacturer's direction)
Blackberries: 1.0 lb. (frozen, thawed, and semi-crushed)
Raspberries: 0.25 lbs. (frozen, thawed, and semi-crushed)
Let sit at cellar or room temperature until clear

Final Racking
Rack mead one final time and let it sit until the mead is clear enough to read through. (Bulk age until ready to bottle)

Directions:
- Before starting, clean and sanitize all of your equipment

Must Preparation
- Pour 2 quarts of water into a large stock pot and bring to a low boil
- Remove from the heat and blend in the honey, stirring until it is completely dissolved
- Add additional water to bring total volume to 1 gallon
- Allow must to cool to room temperature then take a gravity reading
- Pour the cooled must into a 2 gallon brewing bucket and cover with a sanitary cloth and a large rubber band

Yeast Starter
- Mix GoFerm with 50 ml of hot water
- Allow mixture to cool to 104F then add your yeast and stir until dissolved
- Let this mixture sit for 15-20 minutes to allow it to activate

Primary
- When the temperature of the yeast starter drops to within 10 degrees of the must, pour it into the primary bucket and stir it thoroughly to disperse
- Add Blueberries and Cherries
- Add nutrients (Fermaid-O) as directed above
- Add Pectic Enzyme: per manufacturer's direction
- Aerate must twice daily until 1/3 sugar break then once daily until 2/3 sugar break
- When SG reaches target FG, add Sodium Metabisuphite and Potassium Sorbate to kill any remaining yeast and stabilize the must
- Set aside in a cool place until mead clears and fruit loses its color (turns white)
- Rack to secondary

Secondary
- Rack primary must into a clean glass carboy leaving the spent fruit most of the sediment behind
- Add blackberries and raspberries
- Add an airlock and leave in secondary until it clears and fruit loses its color (turns white)

Final Racking
- Rack mead one final time and let it sit until the mead is clear enough to read through (Bulk age until ready to bottle)

Blackberry-Blueberry "Semi-Sweet" Mead

Yield: 1 gallon   OG: 1.106   FG: 1.015   ABV: 12%
Starting Brix: 25.17   Final Brix: 3.83

Primary

Yeast: 2 grams, Lalvin, 71B-1122

GoFerm: 2.50 grams

Nutrients: 1.89 grams Fermaid-O (0.47 grams each at 24, 48, 72 hours after pitching yeast. 4th dose to be administered at either the 1/3 sugar break or on 7th day)

Pectic Enzyme: per manufacturer's direction

Blueberries: 1.5 lbs. (frozen, thawed, and semi-crushed)

Cranberry Honey: 2.96 lbs.

Secondary

Sodium Metabisuphite and Potassium Sorbate (per manufacturer's direction)

Blackberries: 0.5 lbs. (frozen, thawed, and semi-crushed)

Let sit at cellar or room temperature until clear

Final Racking

Rack mead one final time and let it sit until the mead is clear enough to read through. (Bulk age until ready to bottle)

Directions:

- Before starting, clean and sanitize all of your equipment

Must Preparation

- Pour 2 quarts of water into a large stock pot and bring to a low boil
- Remove from the heat and blend in the honey, stirring until it is completely dissolved
- Add additional water to bring total volume to 1 gallon
- Allow must to cool to room temperature then take a gravity reading
- Pour the cooled must into a 2 gallon brewing bucket and cover with a sanitary cloth and a large rubber band

Yeast Starter

- Mix GoFerm with 50 ml of hot water
- Allow mixture to cool to 104F then add your yeast and stir until dissolved
- Let this mixture sit for 15-20 minutes to allow it to activate

Primary

- When the temperature of the yeast starter drops to within 10 degrees of the must, pour it into the primary bucket and stir it thoroughly to disperse
- Add Blueberries
- Add nutrients (Fermaid-O) as directed above
- Add Pectic Enzyme: per manufacturer's direction
- Aerate must twice daily until 1/3 sugar break then once daily until 2/3 sugar break
- When SG reaches target FG, add Sodium Metabisuphite and Potassium Sorbate to kill any remaining yeast and stabilize the must
- Set aside in a cool place until mead clears and fruit loses its color (turns white)
- Rack to secondary

Secondary

- Rack primary must into a clean glass carboy leaving the spent fruit most of the sediment behind
- Add blackberries and an airlock
- Leave in secondary until it clears and fruit loses its color (turns white)

Final Racking

- Rack mead one final time and let it sit until the mead is clear enough to read through (Bulk age until ready to bottle)

Blueberry - Black Currant Mead

Yield: 1 gallon   OG: 1.106   FG: 1.015   ABV: 12%

Starting Brix: 25.17   Final Brix: 3.83

Primary
Yeast: 2 grams, Lalvin 71B-1122
GoFerm: 2.50 grams
Nutrients: 3.78 grams Fermaid-O (0.47 grams each at 24, 48, 72, & 96 hours after pitching yeast.)
Cranberry Honey: 2.90 lbs.
Blueberries: 1.5 lbs. (frozen, thawed, & semi-crushed)
Black Currants: 0.5 lbs. (frozen, thawed, & semi-crushed)
Pectic Enzyme: per manufacturer's direction

Secondary
Sodium Metabisuphite and Potassium Sorbate (per manufacturer's direction)
Let sit at cellar or room temperature until clear

Final Racking
Rack mead one final time and let it sit until the mead is clear enough to read through. (Bulk age until ready to bottle)

"LET THERE BE MELOMELS!" BY ROBERT RATLIFF

Directions:
- Before starting, clean and sanitize all of your equipment

Must Preparation
- Pour 2 quarts of water into a large stock pot and bring to a low boil
- Remove from the heat and blend in the honey, stirring until it is completely dissolved
- Add additional water to bring total volume to 1 gallon
- Allow must to cool to room temperature then take a gravity reading
- Pour the cooled must into a 2 gallon brewing bucket and cover with a sanitary cloth and a large rubber band

Yeast Starter
- Mix GoFerm with 50 ml of hot water
- Allow mixture to cool to 104F then add your yeast and stir until dissolved
- Let this mixture sit for 15-20 minutes to allow it to activate and grow into a nice healthy colony

Primary
- When the temperature of the yeast starter drops to within 10 degrees of the must, pour it into the primary bucket and stir it thoroughly to disperse
- Add Blueberries & Black Currants
- Add Pectic Enzyme: per manufacturer's direction
- Add nutrients (Fermaid-O) as directed above
- Aerate must twice daily until 1/3 sugar break then once daily until 2/3 sugar break

Secondary
- On day ten (10), strain must (through a sieve) into a clean glass carboy to remove the skins
- Add an airlock
- When target gravity is reached, add Sodium Metabisuphite and Potassium Sorbate to kill any remaining yeast
- Leave in secondary until it clears

Final Racking
- Rack mead one final time then bulk age until ready to bottle

Blueberry-Blackberry-Raspberry-Sour Cherry Mead

Yield: 1 gallon   OG: 1.106   FG: 1.015   ABV: 12%

Starting Brix: 25.17   Final Brix: 3.83

Primary

Yeast: 2 grams, Lalvin, 71B-1122
GoFerm: 2.50 grams
Nutrients: 1.89 grams Fermaid-O (0.47 grams each at 24, 48, 72 hours after pitching yeast. 4th dose to be administered at either the 1/3 sugar break or on 7th day)
Pectic Enzyme: per manufacturer's direction
Blueberries: 0.5 lbs. (frozen, thawed, and semi-crushed)
Sour Cherries: 0.75 lbs. (frozen, thawed, and semi-crushed)
Wildflower Honey: 2.98 lbs.

Secondary

Sodium Metabisuphite and Potassium Sorbate (per manufacturer's direction)
Blackberries: 1.0 lb. (frozen, thawed, and semi-crushed)
Raspberries: 0.25 lbs. (frozen, thawed, and semi-crushed)
Let sit at cellar or room temperature until clear

Final Racking

Rack mead one final time and let it sit until the mead is clear enough to read through. (Bulk age until ready to bottle)

Directions:

- Before starting, clean and sanitize all of your equipment

Must Preparation

- Pour 2 quarts of water into a large stock pot and bring to a low boil
- Remove from the heat and blend in the honey, stirring until it is completely dissolved
- Add additional water to bring total volume to 1 gallon
- Allow must to cool to room temperature then take a gravity reading
- Pour the cooled must into a 2 gallon brewing bucket and cover with a sanitary cloth and a large rubber band

Yeast Starter

- Mix GoFerm with 50 ml of hot water
- Allow mixture to cool to 104F then add your yeast and stir until dissolved
- Let this mixture sit for 15-20 minutes to allow it to activate and grow into a nice healthy colony

Primary

- When the temperature of the yeast starter drops to within 10 degrees of the must, pour it into the primary bucket and stir it thoroughly to disperse
- Add Blueberries and Cherries
- Add nutrients (Fermaid-O) as directed above
- Add Pectic Enzyme: per manufacturer's direction
- Aerate must twice daily until 1/3 sugar break then once daily until 2/3 sugar break
- When SG reaches target FG, add Sodium Metabisuphite and Potassium Sorbate to kill any remaining yeast and stabilize the must
- Set aside in a cool place until mead clears and fruit loses its color (turns white)
- Rack to secondary

Secondary

- Rack primary must into a clean glass carboy leaving the spent fruit most of the sediment behind
- Add blackberries and raspberries
- Add an airlock
- Leave in secondary until it clears and fruit loses its color (turns white)

Final Racking

- Rack mead one final time and let it sit until the mead is clear enough to read through (Bulk age until ready to bottle)

Blueberry-Blackberry-Raspberry-Strawberry-Sour Cherry

Yield: 1 gallon   OG: 1.106   FG: 1.015   ABV: 12%
Starting Brix: 25.17   Final Brix: 3.83

Primary

Yeast: 2 grams, Lalvin, 71B-1122

GoFerm: 2.50 grams

Nutrients: 1.89 grams Fermaid-O (0.47 grams each at 24, 48, 72 hours after pitching yeast. 4th dose to be administered at either the 1/3 sugar break or on 7th day)

Cranberry Honey: 3.00 lbs.

Pectic Enzyme: per manufacturer's direction

Blueberries: 0.50 lbs. (frozen, thawed, and semi-crushed)

Strawberries: 0.50 lbs. (frozen, thawed, and semi-crushed)

Sour Cherries: 0.50 lbs. (frozen, thawed, and semi-crushed)

Secondary

Sodium Metabisuphite and Potassium Sorbate (per manufacturer's direction)

Blackberries: 0.25 lbs. (frozen, thawed, and semi-crushed)

Raspberries: 0.25 lbs. (frozen, thawed, and semi-crushed)

Let sit at cellar or room temperature until fruit loses its color (turns white)

Final Racking

Rack mead one final time and let it sit until the mead is clear enough to read through. (Bulk age until ready to bottle)

"LET THERE BE MELOMELS!" BY ROBERT RATLIFF

Directions:
- Before starting, clean and sanitize all of your equipment

Must Preparation
- Pour 2 quarts of water into a large stock pot and bring to a low boil
- Remove from the heat and blend in the honey, stirring until dissolved
- Add additional water to bring total volume to 1 gallon
- Allow must to cool to room temperature then take a gravity reading
- Pour the cooled must into a 2 gallon brewing bucket and cover with a sanitary cloth and a large rubber band

Yeast Starter
- Mix GoFerm with 50 ml of hot water
- Allow mixture to cool to 104F then add your yeast and stir until dissolved
- Let this mixture sit for 15-20 minutes to allow it to activate and grow into a nice healthy colony

Primary
- When the temperature of the yeast starter drops to within 10 degrees of the must, pour it into the primary bucket and stir it thoroughly to disperse
- Add Pectic Enzyme: per manufacturer's direction
- Add Blueberries, Strawberries, & Sour Cherries
- Add nutrients (Fermaid-O) as directed above
- Aerate must twice daily until 1/3 sugar break then once daily until 2/3 sugar break
- When SG reaches target FG, add Sodium Metabisuphite and Potassium Sorbate to kill any remaining yeast and stabilize the must
- Set aside in a cool place until mead clears and fruit loses its color (turns white) then rack to secondary

Secondary
- Rack primary must into a clean glass carboy leaving the spent fruit most of the sediment behind
- Add blackberries and raspberries
- Add an airlock and leave in secondary until fruit loses its color (turns white)

Final Racking
- Rack mead one final time and let it sit until the mead is clear enough to read through (Bulk age until ready to bottle)

Blueberry-Blackberry-Raspberry-Strawberry "Semi-Sweet"

Yield: 1 gallon   OG: 1.106   FG: 1.015   ABV: 12%
Starting Brix: 25.17   Final Brix: 3.83

Primary
Yeast: 2 grams, Lalvin, K1V-1116
GoFerm: 2.50 grams
Nutrients: 1.89 grams Fermaid-O (0.47 grams each at 24, 48, 72 hours after pitching yeast. 4th dose to be administered at either the 1/3 sugar break or on 7th day)
Cranberry Honey: 2.96 lbs.
Pectic Enzyme: per manufacturer's direction
Blueberries: 0.75 lbs. (frozen, thawed, and semi-crushed)
Strawberries: 0.75 lbs. (frozen, thawed, and semi-crushed)

Secondary
Sodium Metabisuphite and Potassium Sorbate (per manufacturer's direction)
Blackberries: 0.25 lbs. (frozen, thawed, and semi-crushed)
Raspberries: 0.25 lbs. (frozen, thawed, and semi-crushed)
Let sit at cellar or room temperature until fruit loses its color (turns white)

Final Racking
Rack mead one final time and let it sit until the mead is clear enough to read through. (Bulk age until ready to bottle)

Directions:
- Before starting, clean and sanitize all of your equipment

Must Preparation
- Pour 2 quarts of water into a large stock pot and bring to a low boil
- Remove from the heat and blend in the honey, stirring until it is completely dissolved
- Add additional water to bring total volume to 1 gallon
- Allow must to cool to room temperature then take a gravity reading
- Pour the cooled must into a 2 gallon brewing bucket and cover with a sanitary cloth and a large rubber band

Yeast Starter
- Mix GoFerm with 50 ml of hot water
- Allow mixture to cool to 104F then add your yeast and stir until dissolved
- Let this mixture sit for 15-20 minutes to allow it to activate and grow into a nice healthy colony

Primary
- When the temperature of the yeast starter drops to within 10 degrees of the must, pour it into the primary bucket and stir it thoroughly to disperse
- Add Pectic Enzyme: per manufacturer's direction
- Add Blueberries & Strawberries
- Add nutrients (Fermaid-O) as directed above
- Aerate must twice daily until 1/3 sugar break then once daily until 2/3 sugar break
- When SG reaches target FG, add Sodium Metabisuphite and Potassium Sorbate to kill any remaining yeast and stabilize the must
- Set aside in a cool place until mead clears and fruit loses its color (turns white)
- Rack to secondary

Secondary
- Rack primary must into a clean glass carboy leaving the spent fruit most of the sediment behind
- Add blackberries and raspberries
- Add Sodium Metabisuphite and Potassium Sorbate to kill any remaining yeast and stabilize the must
- Add an airlock
- Leave in secondary until fruit loses its color (turns white)

Final Racking
- Rack mead one final time and let it sit until the mead is clear enough to read through (Bulk age until ready to bottle)

Coconut Melomel

Yield: 1 gallon   OG: 1.106   FG: 1.015   ABV: 12%
Starting Brix: 25.17   Final Brix: 3.83

Primary

Yeast: 2 grams, Lalvin, 71B-1122
GoFerm: 2.50 grams
Nutrients: 1.89 grams Fermaid-O (0.47 grams each at 24, 48, 72 hours after pitching yeast. 4th dose to be administered at either the 1/3 sugar break or on 7th day)
Wildflower Honey: 3.06 lbs.

Secondary

Sodium Metabisuphite and Potassium Sorbate (per manufacturer's direction)
Coconut, Fresh: 1 lb. (shredded then toasted until lightly browned)
Pectic Enzyme: per manufacturer's direction
Let sit at cellar or room temperature until clear

Final Racking

Rack mead one final time and let it sit until the mead is clear enough to read through. (Bulk age until ready to bottle)

"LET THERE BE MELOMELS!" BY ROBERT RATLIFF

Directions:
- Before starting, clean and sanitize all of your equipment

Must Preparation
- Pour 2 quarts of water into a large stock pot and bring to a low boil
- Remove from the heat and blend in the honey, stirring until it is completely dissolved
- Add additional water to bring total volume to 1 gallon
- Allow must to cool to room temperature then take a gravity reading
- Pour the cooled must into a 2 gallon brewing bucket and cover with a sanitary cloth and a large rubber band

Yeast Starter
- Mix GoFerm with 50 ml of hot water
- Allow mixture to cool to 104F then add your yeast and stir until dissolved
- Let this mixture sit for 15-20 minutes to allow it to activate

Primary
- When the temperature of the yeast starter drops to within 10 degrees of the must, pour it into the primary bucket and stir it thoroughly to disperse
- Add nutrients (Fermaid-O) as directed above
- Aerate must twice daily until 1/3 sugar break then once daily until 2/3 sugar break
- When OG reaches target FG, rack to secondary

Secondary
- Rack primary must into a clean glass carboy over Sodium Metabisuphite and Potassium Sorbate to kill any remaining yeast and leave most of the sediment behind
- Add toasted coconut and an airlock and leave in secondary until mead clears
- Add Pectic Enzyme: per manufacturer's direction

Final Racking
- Rack mead one final time and let it sit until the mead is clear enough to read through (Bulk age until ready to bottle)

Cranberry-Raspberry "Semi-Sweet" Mead

Yield: 1 gallon   OG: 1.106   FG: 1.015   ABV: 12%
Starting Brix: 25.17   Final Brix: 3.83

Primary
Yeast: 2 grams, Lalvin, 71B-1122
GoFerm: 2.50 grams
Nutrients: 1.89 grams Fermaid-O (0.47 grams each at 24, 48, 72 hours after pitching yeast. 4th dose to be administered at either the 1/3 sugar break or on 7th day)
Cranberry Honey: 3.02 lbs.
Cranberries: 0.75 lbs.
Pectic Enzyme: per manufacturer's direction
Sodium Metabisuphite and Potassium Sorbate (per manufacturer's direction)

Secondary
Raspberries: 0.50 lbs.
Let sit at cellar or room temperature until clear

Final Racking
Rack mead one final time and let it sit until the mead is clear enough to read through. (Bulk age until ready to bottle)

Directions:
- Before starting, clean and sanitize all of your equipment

Must Preparation
- Pour 2 quarts of water into a large stock pot and bring to a low boil
- Add cranberries and stir until they are fully blanched
- Remove from the heat and blend in the honey, stirring until it is completely dissolved
- Add additional water to bring total volume to 1 gallon
- Allow must to cool to room temperature then take a gravity reading
- Pour the cooled must into a 2 gallon brewing bucket and cover with a sanitary cloth and a large rubber band

Yeast Starter
- Mix GoFerm with 50 ml of hot water
- Allow mixture to cool to 104F then add your yeast and stir until dissolved
- Let this mixture sit for 15-20 minutes to allow it to activate and grow into a nice healthy colony

Primary
- When the temperature of the yeast starter drops to within 10 degrees of the must, pour it into the primary bucket and stir it thoroughly to disperse
- Add Pectic Enzyme: per manufacturer's direction
- Add nutrients (Fermaid-O) as directed above
- Aerate must twice daily until 1/3 sugar break then once daily until 2/3 sugar break
- When SG reaches target FG, add Sodium Metabisuphite and Potassium Sorbate to stabilize the must and stop fermentation
- Set aside for a total of 1 month from pitching yeast
- Rack to secondary

Secondary
- Rack primary must into a clean glass carboy leaving the fruit and sediment behind
- Add raspberries (frozen, thawed and lightly crushed
- Swirl thoroughly and add an airlock and leave in secondary until it clears and fruit loses its color

Final Racking
- Rack mead one final time and let it sit until the mead is clear enough to read through (Bulk age until ready to bottle)

Elderberry-Blackberry "Sack" Mead

Yield: 1 gallon   OG: 1.157   FG: 1.035   ABV: 16%

Starting Brix: 35.69   Final Brix: 8.78

Primary
Yeast: 2 grams, Lalvin, K1V-1116
GoFerm: 2.50 grams
Nutrients: 2.68 grams Fermaid-O (0.67 grams each at 24, 48, 72 hours after pitching yeast. 4th dose to be administered at either the 1/3 sugar break or on 7th day)
Pectic Enzyme: per manufacturer's direction
Cranberry Honey: 4.30 lbs.
Fresh Elderberries: 2 lbs. (frozen, thawed, & semi-crushed)

Secondary
Sodium Metabisuphite and Potassium Sorbate (per manufacturer's direction)
Fresh Blackberries: 1 lb. (frozen, thawed, & semi-crushed)
Let sit at cellar or room temperature until fruit turns white

Final Racking
Rack mead one final time and let it sit until the mead is clear enough to read through. (Bulk age until ready to bottle)

Directions:
- Before starting, clean and sanitize all of your equipment

Must Preparation
- Pour 2 quarts of water into a large stock pot and bring to a low boil
- Remove from the heat and blend in the honey, stirring until it is completely dissolved
- Add additional water to bring total volume to 1 gallon
- Allow must to cool to room temperature then take a gravity reading
- Pour the cooled must into a 2 gallon brewing bucket and cover with a sanitary cloth and a large rubber band

Yeast Starter
- Mix GoFerm with 50 ml of hot water
- Allow mixture to cool to 104F then add your yeast and stir until dissolved
- Let this mixture sit for 15-20 minutes to allow it to activate and grow into a nice healthy colony

Primary
- When the temperature of the yeast starter drops to within 10 degrees of the must, pour it into the primary bucket and stir it thoroughly to disperse
- Add Elderberries
- Add nutrients (Fermaid-O) as directed above
- Add Pectic Enzyme: per manufacturer's direction
- Aerate must twice daily until 1/3 sugar break then once daily until 2/3 sugar break
- When SG reaches target FG, rack to secondary

Secondary
- Rack primary must into a clean glass carboy over Sodium Metabisuphite and Potassium Sorbate to kill any remaining yeast and leave most of the sediment behind
- Add Blackberries
- Add an airlock
- Leave in secondary until it clears and fruit turns white

Final Racking
- Rack mead one final time and let it sit until the mead is clear enough to read through (Bulk age until ready to bottle)

Orange - Mango "Semi-Sweet" Mead

Yield: 1 gallon   OG: 1.106   FG: 1.015   ABV: 12%
Starting Brix: 25.17   Final Brix: 3.83

Primary

Yeast: 2 grams, Lalvin, D-47
GoFerm: 2.50 grams
Nutrients: 1.89 grams Fermaid-O (0.47 grams each at 24, 48, 72 hours after pitching yeast. 4th dose to be administered at either the 1/3 sugar break or on 7th day)
Pectic Enzyme: per manufacturer's direction
Oranges: 1.0 lbs. (zest, juice, and segmented fruit)
Mango: 0.75 lbs. (frozen, thawed, and semi-crushed)
Orange Blossom Honey: 2.84 lbs.

Secondary

Sodium Metabisuphite and Potassium Sorbate (per manufacturer's direction)
Let sit at cellar or room temperature until clear

Final Racking

Rack mead one final time and let it sit until the mead is clear enough to read through. (Bulk age until ready to bottle)

Directions:
- Before starting, clean and sanitize all of your equipment

Must Preparation
- Pour 2 quarts of water into a large stock pot and bring to a low boil
- Remove from the heat and blend in the honey, stirring until it is completely dissolved
- Add additional water to bring total volume to 1 gallon
- Allow must to cool to room temperature then take a gravity reading
- Pour the cooled must into a 2 gallon brewing bucket and cover with a sanitary cloth and a large rubber band

Yeast Starter
- Mix GoFerm with 50 ml of hot water
- Allow mixture to cool to 104F then add your yeast and stir until dissolved
- Let this mixture sit for 15-20 minutes to allow it to activate and grow into a nice healthy colony

Primary
- When the temperature of the yeast starter drops to within 10 degrees of the must, pour it into the primary bucket and stir it thoroughly to disperse
- Add fruit as directed
- Add nutrients (Fermaid-O) as directed above
- Add Pectic Enzyme: per manufacturer's direction
- Aerate must twice daily until 1/3 sugar break then once daily until 2/3 sugar break
- When SG reaches target FG, add Sodium Metabisuphite and Potassium Sorbate to kill any remaining yeast and stabilize the must
- Set aside in a cool place until mead clears and fruit falls
- Rack to secondary

Secondary
- Rack primary must into a clean glass carboy leaving the spent fruit most of the sediment behind
- Add an airlock
- Leave in secondary until it clears and fruit loses its color (turns white)

Final Racking
- Rack mead one final time and let it sit until the mead is clear enough to read through (Bulk age until ready to bottle)

Orange-Pineapple-Coconut (Escape to the Tropics)

Yield: 1 gallon   OG: 1.106   FG: 1.015   ABV: 12%

Starting Brix: 25.17   Final Brix: 3.83

Primary

Yeast: 2 grams, Lalvin, ICV-D47

GoFerm: 2.50 grams

Nutrients: 1.89 grams Fermaid-O (0.47 grams each at 24, 48, 72 hours after pitching yeast. 4th dose to be administered at either the 1/3 sugar break or on 7th day)

Orange Blossom Honey: 2.90 lbs.

Coconut, Fresh: ½ lb. (shredded then toasted until lightly browned)

Pineapple: 1 lb. cut into chunks

Pectic Enzyme: per manufacturer's direction

Secondary

Sodium Metabisuphite and Potassium Sorbate (per manufacturer's direction)

Orange: 1 (juice and zest)

Let sit at cellar or room temperature until clear

Final Racking

Rack mead one final time and let it sit until the mead is clear enough to read through. (Bulk age until ready to bottle)

Directions:
- Before starting, clean and sanitize all of your equipment

Must Preparation
- Pour 2 quarts of water into a large stock pot and bring to a low boil
- Remove from the heat and blend in the honey, stirring until it is completely dissolved
- Add additional water to bring total volume to 1 gallon
- Allow must to cool to room temperature then take a gravity reading
- Pour the cooled must into a 2 gallon brewing bucket and cover with a sanitary cloth and a large rubber band

Yeast Starter
- Mix GoFerm with 50 ml of hot water
- Allow mixture to cool to 104F then add your yeast and stir until dissolved
- Let this mixture sit for 15-20 minutes to allow it to activate and grow into a nice healthy colony

Primary
- When the temperature of the yeast starter drops to within 10 degrees of the must, pour it into the primary bucket and stir it thoroughly to disperse
- Add pineapple chunks and toasted coconut
- Add Pectic Enzyme: per manufacturer's direction
- Add nutrients (Fermaid-O) as directed above
- Aerate must twice daily until 1/3 sugar break then once daily until 2/3 sugar break
- When SG reaches target FG, rack to secondary

Secondary
- Rack primary must into a clean glass carboy over Sodium Metabisuphite and Potassium Sorbate to kill any remaining yeast and leave most of the sediment behind
- Add juice and zest from one orange
- Add an airlock
- Leave in secondary until it clears

Final Racking
- Rack mead one final time and let it sit until the mead is clear enough to read through (Bulk age until ready to bottle)

Orange - Pineapple Melomel

Yield: 1 gallon   OG: 1.106   FG: 1.015   ABV: 12%
Starting Brix: 25.17   Final Brix: 3.83

Primary

Yeast: 2 grams, Lalvin, D-47

GoFerm: 2.50 grams

Nutrients: 1.89 grams Fermaid-O (0.47 grams each at 24, 48, 72 hours after pitching yeast. 4th dose to be administered at either the 1/3 sugar break or on 7th day)

Orange Blossom Honey: 2.89 lbs.

Orange: 0.75 lbs. (zest and sectioned fruit w/o pith)

Pineapple: 0.75 lbs. cut into chunks

Pectic Enzyme: per manufacturer's direction

Sodium Metabisuphite and Potassium Sorbate (per manufacturer's direction)

Secondary

Let sit at cellar or room temperature until clear

Final Racking

Rack mead one final time and let it sit until the mead is clear enough to read through. (Bulk age until ready to bottle)

Directions:
- Before starting, clean and sanitize all of your equipment

Must Preparation
- Pour 2 quarts of water into a large stock pot and bring to a low boil
- Remove from the heat and blend in the honey, stirring until it is completely dissolved
- Add additional water to bring total volume to 1 gallon
- Allow must to cool to room temperature then take a gravity reading
- Pour the cooled must into a 2 gallon brewing bucket and cover with a sanitary cloth and a large rubber band

Yeast Starter
- Mix GoFerm with 50 ml of hot water
- Allow mixture to cool to 104F then add your yeast and stir until dissolved
- Let this mixture sit for 15-20 minutes to allow it to activate and grow into a nice healthy colony

Primary
- When the temperature of the yeast starter drops to within 10 degrees of the must, pour it into the primary bucket and stir it thoroughly to disperse
- Add pineapple chunks, orange slices, and zest
- Add Pectic Enzyme: per manufacturer's direction
- Add nutrients (Fermaid-O) as directed above
- Aerate must twice daily until 1/3 sugar break then once daily until 2/3 sugar break
- When SG reaches target FG add Sodium Metabisuphite and Potassium Sorbate to kill any remaining yeast and stabilize the mead
- Leave in secondary for 1 month then rack to secondary

Secondary
- Rack primary must into a clean glass carboy leaving most of the sediment behind
- Add an airlock
- Leave in secondary until it clears completely

Final Racking
- Rack mead one final time and let it sit until the mead is clear enough to read through (Bulk age until ready to bottle)

Orange – Raspberry "Semi-Sweet" Melomel

Yield: 1 gallon   OG: 1.106   FG: 1.015   ABV: 12%

Starting Brix: 25.17   Final Brix: 3.83

Primary

Yeast: 2 grams, Lalvin, D-47

GoFerm: 2.50 grams

Nutrients: 1.89 grams Fermaid-O (0.47 grams each at 24, 48, 72 hours after pitching yeast. 4th dose to be administered at either the 1/3 sugar break or on 7th day)

Pectic Enzyme: per manufacturer's direction

Oranges: 1.0 lb. (zest, juice, and segmented fruit)

Orange Blossom Honey: 2.98 lbs.

Secondary

Sodium Metabisuphite and Potassium Sorbate (per manufacturer's direction)

Raspberries: 0.25 lbs. (frozen, thawed, and semi-crushed)

Let sit at cellar or room temperature until clear

Final Racking

Rack mead one final time and let it sit until the mead is clear enough to read through. (Bulk age until ready to bottle)

Directions:
- Before starting, clean and sanitize all of your equipment

Must Preparation
- Pour 2 quarts of water into a large stock pot and bring to a low boil
- Remove from the heat and blend in the honey, stirring until it is completely dissolved
- Add additional water to bring total volume to 1 gallon
- Allow must to cool to room temperature then take a gravity reading
- Pour the cooled must into a 2 gallon brewing bucket and cover with a sanitary cloth and a large rubber band

Yeast Starter
- Mix GoFerm with 50 ml of hot water
- Allow mixture to cool to 104F then add your yeast and stir until dissolved
- Let this mixture sit for 15-20 minutes to allow it to activate and grow into a nice healthy colony

Primary
- When the temperature of the yeast starter drops to within 10 degrees of the must, pour it into the primary bucket and stir it thoroughly to disperse
- Add Oranges (zest, juice, and segmented fruit)
- Add nutrients (Fermaid-O) as directed above
- Add Pectic Enzyme: per manufacturer's direction
- Aerate must twice daily until 1/3 sugar break then once daily until 2/3 sugar break
- When SG reaches target FG, add Sodium Metabisuphite and Potassium Sorbate to kill any remaining yeast and stabilize the must
- Set aside in a cool place until mead clears and fruit falls
- Rack to secondary

Secondary
- Rack primary must into a clean glass carboy leaving the spent fruit most of the sediment behind
- Add raspberries (frozen, thawed, and semi-crushed)
- Add an airlock
- Leave in secondary until it clears and fruit loses its color (turns white)

Final Racking
- Rack mead one final time and let it sit until the mead is clear enough to read through (Bulk age until ready to bottle)

Pineapple – Sour Cherry "Sweet" Mead

Yield: 1 gallon   OG: 1.132   FG: 1.025   ABV: 14%
Starting Brix: 30.53   Final Brix: 6.33

Primary

Yeast: 2 grams, Lalvin, D-47
1.5 lbs. Fresh Pineapple (grilled or roasted to caramelize the sugars)
0.5 lbs. Sour Cherries
GoFerm: 2.50 grams
Nutrients: 2.29 grams Fermaid-O (0.57 grams each at 24, 48, 72 hours after pitching yeast. 4th dose to be administered at either the 1/3 sugar break or on 7th day)
Pectic Enzyme: per manufacturer's direction
Cranberry Honey: 3.53 lbs.

Secondary

Sodium Metabisuphite and Potassium Sorbate (per manufacturer's direction)
Let sit at cellar or room temperature until clear

Final Racking

Rack mead one final time and let it sit until the mead is clear enough to read through. (Bulk age until ready to bottle)

Directions:
- Before starting, clean and sanitize all of your equipment

Must Preparation
- Pour 2 quarts of water into a large stock pot and bring to a low boil
- Remove from the heat and blend in the honey, stirring until it is completely dissolved
- Add additional water to bring total volume to 1 gallon
- Allow must to cool to room temperature then take a gravity reading
- Pour the cooled must into a 2 gallon brewing bucket and cover with a sanitary cloth and a large rubber band

Yeast Starter
- Mix GoFerm with 50 ml of hot water
- Allow mixture to cool to 104F then add your yeast and stir until dissolved
- Let this mixture sit for 15-20 minutes to allow it to activate and grow into a nice healthy colony

Primary
- When the temperature of the yeast starter drops to within 10 degrees of the must, pour it into the primary bucket and stir it thoroughly to disperse
- Add fruit as directed (Freeze, thaw, and semi-crush fruit before adding to primary)
- Add nutrients (Fermaid-O) as directed above
- Add Pectic Enzyme: per manufacturer's direction
- Aerate must twice daily until 1/3 sugar break then once daily until 2/3 sugar break
- When OG reaches target FG, rack to secondary

Secondary
- Rack primary must into a clean glass carboy over Sodium Metabisuphite and Potassium Sorbate to kill any remaining yeast and leave most of the sediment behind
- Add an airlock and set aside until mead clears

Final Racking
- Rack mead one final time and let it sit until the mead is clear enough to read through (Bulk age until ready to bottle)

Pineapple Melomel "Semi-Sweet"

Yield: 1 gallon   OG: 1.106   FG: 1.015   ABV: 12%
Starting Brix: 25.17   Final Brix: 3.83

Primary

Yeast: 2 grams, Lalvin, ICV-D47

GoFerm: 2.50 grams

Nutrients: 1.89 grams Fermaid-O (0.47 grams each at 24, 48, 72 hours after pitching yeast. 4th dose to be administered at either the 1/3 sugar break or on 7th day)

Orange Blossom Honey: 2.94 lbs.

Fresh Pineapple: 1 lb. (chucked, frozen, thawed, & slightly crushed)

Pectic Enzyme: per manufacturer's direction

Secondary

Sodium Metabisuphite and Potassium Sorbate (per manufacturer's direction)

Let sit at cellar or room temperature until clear

Final Racking

Rack mead one final time and let it sit until the mead is clear enough to read through. (Bulk age until ready to bottle)

Directions:
- Before starting, clean and sanitize all of your equipment

Must Preparation
- Pour 2 quarts of water into a large stock pot and bring to a low boil
- Remove from the heat and blend in the honey, stirring until it is completely dissolved
- Add additional water to bring total volume to 1 gallon
- Allow must to cool to room temperature then take a gravity reading
- Pour the cooled must into a 2 gallon brewing bucket and cover with a sanitary cloth and a large rubber band

Yeast Starter
- Mix GoFerm with 50 ml of hot water
- Allow mixture to cool to 104F then add your yeast and stir until dissolved
- Let this mixture sit for 15-20 minutes to allow it to activate and grow into a nice healthy colony

Primary
- When the temperature of the yeast starter drops to within 10 degrees of the must, pour it into the primary bucket and stir it thoroughly to disperse
- Add the pineapple chunks
- Add Pectic Enzyme: per manufacturer's direction
- Add nutrients (Fermaid-O) as directed above
- Aerate must twice daily until 1/3 sugar break then once daily until 2/3 sugar break
- When SG reaches target FG, rack to secondary

Secondary
- Rack primary must into a clean glass carboy over Sodium Metabisuphite and Potassium Sorbate to kill any remaining yeast and leave most of the sediment behind
- Add an airlock
- Leave in secondary until it clears

Final Racking
- Rack mead one final time and let it sit until the mead is clear enough to read through (Bulk age until ready to bottle)

Pineapple-Mango Melomel "Semi-Sweet"

Yield: 1 gallon   OG: 1.106   FG: 1.015   ABV: 12%
Starting Brix: 25.17   Final Brix: 3.83

Primary

Yeast: 2 grams, Lalvin, ICV-D47
GoFerm: 2.50 grams
Nutrients: 1.89 grams Fermaid-O (0.47 grams each at 24, 48, 72 hours after pitching yeast. 4th dose to be administered at either the 1/3 sugar break or on 7th day)
Orange Blossom Honey: 2.76 lbs.
Fresh Pineapple: 1 lb. (chunked, frozen, thawed, & slightly crushed)
Fresh Mango: 1 lb. (chunked, frozen, thawed, & slightly crushed)
Pectic Enzyme: per manufacturer's direction

Secondary

Sodium Metabisuphite and Potassium Sorbate (per manufacturer's direction)
Let sit at cellar or room temperature until clear

Final Racking

Rack mead one final time and let it sit until the mead is clear enough to read through. (Bulk age until ready to bottle)

Directions:
- Before starting, clean and sanitize all of your equipment

Must Preparation
- Pour 2 quarts of water into a large stock pot and bring to a low boil
- Remove from the heat and blend in the honey, stirring until it is completely dissolved
- Add additional water to bring total volume to 1 gallon
- Allow must to cool to room temperature then take a gravity reading
- Pour the cooled must into a 2 gallon brewing bucket and cover with a sanitary cloth and a large rubber band

Yeast Starter
- Mix GoFerm with 50 ml of hot water.
- Allow mixture to cool to 104F then add your yeast and stir until dissolved.
- Let this mixture sit for 15-20 minutes to allow it to activate and grow into a nice healthy colony.

Primary
- When the temperature of the yeast starter drops to within 10 degrees of the must, pour it into the primary bucket and stir it thoroughly to disperse.
- Add the slightly crushed fruit.
- Add Pectic Enzyme: per manufacturer's direction
- Add nutrients (Fermaid-O) as directed above.
- Aerate must twice daily until 1/3 sugar break then once daily until 2/3 sugar break.
- When SG reaches target FG, rack to secondary.

Secondary
- Rack primary must into a clean glass carboy over Sodium Metabisuphite and Potassium Sorbate to kill any remaining yeast and leave most of the sediment behind.
- Add an airlock.
- Leave in secondary until it clears.

Final Racking
- Rack mead one final time and let it sit until the mead is clear enough to read through (Bulk age until ready to bottle)

Strawberry - Kiwi "Semi-Sweet" Melomel

Yield: 1 gallon   OG: 1.106   FG: 1.015   ABV: 12%
Starting Brix: 25.17   Final Brix: 3.83

Primary
Yeast: 2 grams, Lalvin, K1V-1116
GoFerm: 2.50 grams
Kiwi: 2 lbs. (peeled, sliced, frozen, and then thawed)
Strawberries: 1 lb. (sliced, frozen, and then thawed)
Pectic Enzyme: per manufacturer's direction
Nutrients: 1.89 grams Fermaid-O (0.47grams each at 24, 48, 72 hours after pitching yeast. 4th dose to be administered at either the 1/3 sugar break or on 7th day)
Wildflower Honey: 1.86 lbs.

Secondary
Sodium Metabisuphite and Potassium Sorbate (per manufacturer's direction)
Let sit at cellar or room temperature until clear

Final Racking
Rack mead one final time and let it sit until the mead is clear enough to read through. (Bulk age until ready to bottle)

"LET THERE BE MELOMELS!" BY ROBERT RATLIFF

Directions:
- Before starting, clean and sanitize all of your equipment

Must Preparation
- Pour 2 quarts of water into a large stock pot and bring to a low boil
- Remove from the heat and blend in the honey, stirring until it is completely dissolved
- Add additional water to bring total volume to 1 gallon
- Allow must to cool to room temperature then take a gravity reading
- Pour the cooled must into a 2 gallon brewing bucket and cover with a sanitary cloth and a large rubber band

Yeast Starter
- Mix GoFerm with 50 ml of hot water
- Allow mixture to cool to 104F then add your yeast and stir until dissolved
- Let this mixture sit for 15-20 minutes to allow it to activate and grow into a nice healthy colony

Primary
- When the temperature of the yeast starter drops to within 10 degrees of the must, pour it into the primary bucket and stir it thoroughly to disperse
- Add kiwi and strawberries
- Add Pectic Enzyme: per manufacturer's direction
- Add nutrients (Fermaid-O) as directed above
- Aerate must twice daily until 1/3 sugar break then once daily until 2/3 sugar break
- When SG reaches target FG, add Sodium Metabisuphite and Potassium Sorbate to kill any remaining yeast and stabilize the must
- Set aside in a cool place until mead clears and fruit loses its color (turns white)
- Rack to secondary

Secondary
- Rack primary must into a clean glass carboy leaving the spent fruit most of the sediment behind
- Add an airlock
- Leave in secondary until it clears

Final Racking
- Rack mead one final time and let it sit until the mead is clear enough to read through (Bulk age until ready to bottle)

M4B – Historical Meads (Polish Melomels)

TYPES & DESCRIPTIONS

In this next section we will delve into one of my own personal favorite types of melomels. No matter who you are in the home brewing community, there's something about a Polish style melomel that piques the interest like few others. I know that when I was first learning how to make meads myself it was always a goal of mine to learn this particular style. Today, after over a decade, I feel that I've gained a certain level of competency, but I still believe that I'm just scratching the surface when it comes to the patience, dedication, and skill level these true masters of the craft exhibit on a regular basis.

Miód Pitny, or "Drinkable Honey" is one of Poland's best-known traditional alcohols. In fact, it's taken so seriously that Polish mead classifications are registered with the European Commission and officially treated as traditional specialty. As such, they are very strictly defined into their various types and the baseline parameters for each are strictly adhered to.

Polish meads are classified primarily by their honey to water ratios and starting/finishing Brix ranges. What follows is a listing of those classifications and what defines them. The ratios are the critical element in this process. I have broken two of these classifications down by Brix and Specific Gravity to assist you the home brewer in better understanding them. This will help you to develop your own Polish mead recipes as you progress.

"The division of traditional Polish meads based on the density of the must."

The four main categories of Polish meads are listed below.

Półtorak meads are made from one part honey to one half part water (1 : 1/2). These heavy gravity meads are typically difficult to ferment. One way to attempt to make this difficult mead is to "step feed" it. This involves adding additional honey to an established fermentation during primary to minimize the strain on the yeast as it works its way through so much honey. These meads require extended aging times ranging between 5-10 years. Some of them might sit in their barrels for up to 25 years before maturing enough to bottle. Typically, the ABV of a Półtorak is between 16-18%.

Dwójniak meads consist of one part honey and one part water (1 : 1). Dwójniak meads are where the Polish product really starts to get interesting. They finish sweet, like a good dessert mead, with a final ABV between 15-16%. Dwójniaks typically have fruit, spice, or herbs added, but the fruit juice additions do result in a longer aging period (roughly 4 years) to blend them with the other flavors of the mead. Sometimes aged on oak, these meads can start to take on the "port" like overtones most people tend to associate with Polish meads.

Trójniak meads consist of one part honey, two parts water (1 : 2). Trójniak meads are a very popular style of Polish mead. This is the "entry level" for higher quality meads in Poland. They finish out at about 13-14% ABV, and are classified as semi-sweet. Quite often, trójniaks will have fruit, spice, or herb additions. Despite their commonalities with American meads of the same sweetness levels, trójniaks do not quite conform to the western idea of a typical melomel. Trojniaks are typically aged 1-2 years minimum but can take longer based on the recipe.

Czwórniak meads use a one part honey to three parts water ratio (1 : 3). This puts them at the lowest initial SG mead on this list. It ferments out at a dry to almost semi-sweet level with roughly an 11% ABV. They're sometimes aged on oak for a short period, but not regularly by any means. This style of mead isn't regarded very highly except by people who enjoy dry meads, even in Poland.

Now that the basics of defining Polish mead styles have been explained a bit, we can get into a bit more depth of detail on the two most commonly found Polish meads. Dwójniak and Trójniak meads are likely the most prolific of the Polish classifications and you're most likely to run across when searching for good Polish meads.

Dwójniak: 1 part by volume of honey and 1 part by volume of water.
Brix: 45-53 (Maturation of about five years)
- Pitch at 40 Brix (SG: 1.179)
- Back sweeten to 16-18 Brix after fermentation ends
- SG: 1.206 – 1.250 (Target = 1.228)
- FG: 1.085 – 1.128 (Target = 1.107)
- Starting Brix: 45 – 53 (Target = 49)
- Finishing Brix: 21 – 30 (Target = 25)
- Final ABV: 15% – 18% (Target = 16%)

Trójniak: 1 part by volume of honey and 2 parts by volume of water.
Brix: 32-37 (Maturation of about 2-3 years)
- SG: 1.139 – 1.164 (Target = 1.152)
- FG: 1.033– 1.058 (Target = 1.045)
- Starting Brix: 32 – 37 (Target = 35)
- Finishing Brix: 8 – 14 (Target = 11)
- Final ABV: 12% – 15% ABV (Target = 14%)

As you can see, I've gone into some detail mapping out the ranges, gravity levels, and Brix numbers for these two types of mead. I did this primarily to show you that when they get down to basics, Polish meads really aren't that different from our own efforts and styles here in the USA or the rest of the world. It's the details of how they're made that truly separate them from the rest of us. This isn't to say that Polish meads are better than the rest of them. Just that they're very well established and have definitely earned their place among traditionally brewed beverages throughout history.

The given name in each classification is the only official nomenclature for honey admitted to commercial trading. Specific ratios of honey to water must be observed to be able to call each mead by its individual classification. In practice, these numbers are used to calculate how much honey you'll need for the entire batch as a whole. You won't start out with all of it in the must at first. Some of the honey will be added during fermentation after Primary is well under weigh.

"LET THERE BE MELOMELS!" BY ROBERT RATLIFF

The following is a list of a few key bullet points to keep in mind when describing (or aspiring to create) Polish style melomels.

- Polish mead classifications are defined using specific honey to water ratios. An example of this would be a Trójniak.
    - Trójniaks by definition equal 1 part honey + 2 parts water.
- Fruits are almost only used in primary fermentation.
- For a Trójniak, your starting Brix calculations should range somewhere between 32 and 37. Find yourself a good yeast strain that will not only compliment your fruit, but also will produce a final ABV of about 14% and finish fermentation between 8 – 14 Brix. In my opinion, this will provide the optimal sweetness range and strength for a Trójniak.
- Aging is very important. A general rule for a homemade Trójniak is to age it for 2 or 3 years. A Dwójniak will typically age for 5 years.
- When making Polish melomels, the ratio system gets a bit tricky due to the residual sugars inherent in the fruits used. Since fruits have their own sugar, a bit of extra care should be taken when starting a batch. You'll need to calculate the amount of sugar in your fruit then subtract that from your total honey volume to offset that difference.
- Using fruits (fresh or frozen) you should count the amount of sugar in them and remove a part of honey from your recipe or to use a refractometer or a hydrometer to measure a starting Brix.
- In Poland the most common way is to make a melomel is to use actual fruit rather than just juices. This provides the mead with a much better taste and color extraction while also providing a bit of tannin to the mix from the skins.
- The most popular fruits used in Polish meads are sour cherries, black currants, strawberries, raspberries, rosehips, sloes, and bilberries.

By keeping all of these points in mind and doing as much of the math in advance as possible, you can develop some very tasty Polish style meads. Fruit combinations are as common as single fruit meads so let your imagination be a part of your learning process and don't be afraid to try something a bit out of the box once you've learned the basics of the techniques that follow.

DEVELOPING YOUR PRIMARY

Traditionally speaking, Polish melomels are made using either fresh or frozen fruits. They're not big on using fruit juice or puree. In this section, we will go over the basic process of how to prepare your primary for fermentation. This will include a two-step process for primary fermentation that should provide you the tools for a solid foundation toward making your own Polish melomels.

Before I delve into this section, I'll preface it with this small caveat. This process while developed and used actively by several Polish mead makers is not specifically the "Traditional" or "Historical" process Polish mead makers have been using for centuries. This process has been modernized and uses a balance of the old with the new. Additionally, it has produced medal-winning meads for years for the master of the craft who passed this knowledge on to me.

For the first step in this process, you'll want to prepare your initial must. In a clean brewing bucket, make a starter consisting of your crushed fruit, water and honey. For every 3 kilos of fruit, add 1 liter of water. This is a good rule of thumb in general, but it's not carved in stone. Some fruits vary in density so viscosity is a factor. If the must looks too thick, add a bit more water. The main point I'm getting at here being that if you do vary from the baseline, be sure to keep good notes. This tracks what you did and why in case your mead turns out better (or worse) than anticipated. Sometimes the difference between being able to recreate a great mead and possibly losing it forever simply comes down to good record keeping.

Your next step will be to blend enough honey in to this mixture to reach about 20 Brix. You'll need to verify this by using a refractometer. The remaining honey and water allotted for this batch will be added later so be sure to note how much you added here and subtract that from your total amounts.

The next step is to add your rehydrated yeast and Pectic Enzymes. The addition of Pectic Enzymes is critical to the success of this method of primary fermentation.

Without these enzymes, this process will simply not work. Pectic enzymes help to break down both the skins and fruit pulp giving better color and flavor extraction as well as reducing protein haze in your final product. All of this is critical to making good mead. The use of Pectic Enzymes will also assist you by causing the skins and used fruit pulp to float to the surface where it can be more easily removed in step two.

After 1-3 days in primary, it will be time to remove the fruit. This can be done using a slotted spoon and cheesecloth. (Yes, this is step two)

First, you'll need to scoop out the fruits using the slotted spoon and placing them into a press bag for juice extraction. A basic fruit press is probably the most efficient tool for this step but there are other alternatives available if you need to get creative. After pressing, the gathered juice should be poured into a second clean fermentation bucket.

The remaining liquid in your first bucket can now be strained through a clean cheesecloth into the second bucket as well. Straining it through cheesecloth will remove any pits or leftover bits of fruit that might have made it through the slots in your spoon when you scooped out the fruit.

Now that the must has been transferred to this second bucket; it is time to add the remaining water and honey you calculated earlier to finish fermentation. It's very important to remember when adding this remaining honey and water to be sure you subtracted the amount of sugar included in your fruit. For example 10 kilos of fruits has about 1 kilo of sugar, so it is about 1.25 kilos of honey.

Fermenting fruit meads using pectic enzymes is a very efficient method when mead making. During pressing it's quite common to retain between 85-90% of the juice as a direct result of their use. An additional benefit to pressing just 2 or 3 days after the start of fermentation is that the must remain free from any oxidation. Additionally, must processed in this manner is typically so clean that you lose only a minimal amount when racking to secondary.

CONTROLLING ACIDITY (pH)

Fruits used to make melomels have mainly 3 acids: malic, citric and tartaric. All of these will decrease the level of pH (increase the acidity) of the must. This can cause issues with your fermentation because in most cases yeast will stop working if the must drops below a 3.2 on the pH scale. To avoid this, we need to measure the pH of the must before pitching and during a few first days of fermentation. For accurate measurements you'll need to use a digital pH meter, as test strips are not recommended for this instance.

If your must is too acidic, you'll need to correct the level of pH by lowering the acidity levels. Your best options for this will be to use either potassium carbonate K_2CO_3 or potassium bicarbonate $KHCO_3$. Calcium carbonate $CaCO_3$, popular in winemaking will not work properly in this instance.

To adjust the pH of the must, prepare an inoculation of approximately 0.2 gram of potassium per liter of must, remove a bit of the must into a separate container, stir in the $KHCO_3$, pour this mixture back into the main fermenter and re-check your pH again. Repeat as needed until you are between 3.3 - 3.4 on your pH meter.

YEAST REHYDRATION

When preparing your yeast starter for a Polish style mead, the rehydration process is a bit different than you might be used to. As the majority of Polish meads are considered "High-Gravity" you'll need a particularly robust starter to keep your fermentation from stalling on you.

If this will be your first attempt at a Polish style mead, you'll probably want to consider using a "Bayanus" yeast strain. Uvaferm 43, Fermentis BCS103, or Lalvin EC-1118 would all be solid choices to consider. These strains are particularly hearty and will require a bit less attention to finish out properly.

If you've already had some success making this type of mead, then you may want to try using a "Saccharomyces Cerevisiae" type of yeast such as Lalvin's 71B-1122 or D-47 strains. These strains are widely used for fruit wines and meads and will give you a well-defined fruit character. It will also require more work on your part to ferment properly in a high-gravity must.

Trójniaks a rule of thumb will require 1g of yeast per 1 liter of must.
With this in mind, the following would be a good description of how to prepare a yeast starter for a 10-liter batch of Polish Trójniak.

Ingredients:
10 g of yeast
12.5 g of GoFerm
250 ml of boiled water
10 grams of sugar (Saccharomyces Cerevisiae) or 20 grams of sugar (Saccharomyces Bayanus)
**Note the difference in sugar required based on yeast type. This is an important point to starting a healthy batch of yeast depending on which you choose.

Process:
Pour 250 ml of boiled water into a measuring cup
Add the sugar (Stir until completely dissolved)
Cool to 43C then add in the GoFerm (Stir until completely dissolved)
Cool to 38C then add the yeast (Stir until it is mixed in completely)
Rehydrate the yeast for about 20 minutes.
The rehydrated yeast solution should then be cooled slowly until it reaches a temperature between 2-3C of your primary must before pitching.
**Note: This can be easily done by adding a few spoons of must to your yeast starter in roughly 30-minute intervals until the temps are within tolerance.

Following these simple steps should result in a very healthy yeast starter that will dive right into the must and start off your primary in a big way.

POLISH MEAD RECIPES

Finally we get into the Polish mead recipes you've been waiting for. This section will present several medal winning mead recipes, a few non-medal winners, and the potential to open your mind to possibilities limited only by your imagination. I'm particularly excited to be spotlighting the recipes of two extremely talented Polish meadmakers in this section who are rapidly becoming quite well known due to their diligence and level of skill in crafting excellent meads.

Marek Leczycki and Jerzy Kasperski have each been making (and drinking) great meads for years now and they've graciously offered a wonderful selection of their award winning recipes to be included in this installment of my series.

As your own skills making this type of mead develop, I have no doubt you'll occasionally drive yourself to distraction pondering new ideas and what flavor combinations to develop for your next batch.

Due to the inherent difficulties involved in making a Dwójniak strength mead, there will be only one recipe example included in this volume. However, it is a recipe that earned Best of Show at the 2016 Mead Free or Die competition in New Hampshire. Additionally, the process for creating one will be covered in detail so you'll have a sound baseline if you'd like to attempt one of your own devising.

The remaining recipes in this section will all be Trójniak strength. That being said, you'll notice a large number of medal winners among them and I'm confident that you'll get the gist of this style of brewing as you read and learn. I know I did.

In the end, as with my first book, my main purpose aside of providing you with a good selection of recipes to choose from is to inspire new creations and to broaden the spectrum of your own efforts as mead makers.

Trójniak 26
Created by: Marek Łęczycki

Winner: Second Place – Mazer Cup International 2012
Style: M4B Historical (Polish Trójniak)
Style: M2E Other/Mixed Fruit
Batch Yield: ~13.5 liters
ABV: Between 14-16%
Starting Brix: 20

Ingredients
- Brewing Buckets, 15-liter (2 ea.)
- Strawberries: 4 kg
- Bananas: 1 kg (ripe, without skins)
- Acacia honey: 0.5 kg
- Buckwheat honey: 0.5 kg
- Wildflower honey: 4.5 kg
- Water: 6 liters
- Yeast, Lalvin 71B-1122: 10 grams
- Nutrient: Fermaid-O (or Activit-O)
- Nutrient: Diammonium Phosphate (DAP)
- Nutrient: GoFerm
- Pectic Enzyme (Powder): per manufacturer's direction
- Stabilizer: Sodium Metabisulphite
- Stabilizer: Potassium Sorbate

Yeast Starter
- Pour 250 ml of boiled water into a measuring cup
- Add 10 grams of sugar (Stir until completely dissolved)
- Allow starter to cool to 43C (109F) then add in 12.5 grams of GoFerm (Stir until completely dissolved)
- Allow additional time for starter to cool to about 38C (100F) then add the yeast.
- Slowly adjust temp down by adding a spoon of must every few minutes until starter temp is between 2-3C of your primary must before pitching

"LET THERE BE MELOMELS!" BY ROBERT RATLIFF

Directions:

Day One

- Before starting, clean and sanitize all of your equipment.
- Freeze all of the fruit you'll be using for this mead.
- Put the strawberries into a 15-liter primary bucket and allow them to thaw.
- Thoroughly crush the fruit to release as much juice as possible.
- Blend in 0.5 kg of acacia honey.
- Check pH and adjust using Potassium Bicarbonate as directed under "CONTROLLING ACIDITY" until you reach a pH of ~3.4 (Stay above 3.2)
- When the temperature of the yeast starter and must are within a few degrees of tolerance, pitch the yeast and stir thoroughly to disperse it into the must.
- Add first dose of nutrients (Fermaid-O @ 0.4g/l by volume)
- Add Pectic Enzyme: per manufacturer's direction.
- Punch down the cap 2-3 times during the first 24 hours to maximize yeast contact, degas thoroughly, and to keep the fruits wet.

Day Two

- Remove the fruit and press as directed in "DEVELOPING YOUR PRIMARY" pouring the resultant juice into a 15-liter plastic brew bucket (w/airlock).
- Filter the remaining liquid through clean cheesecloth into the carboy as well to remove leftover fruit pieces and particulates. (Yield should be ~3.7 liters)
- Add 6 liters of water.
- Add the balance of the honey. (0.5 kg Buckwheat, 3.7 kg Wildflower, & any remaining Acacia)
- Add second dose of nutrients. (Fermaid-O @ 0.4g/l by volume)

Day Three

- Add the third and final dose of nutrients consisting of the following…
  - 0.4g/liter of Fermaid-O by volume
  - 0.6 g/liter of Diammonium Phosphate (DAP) by volume.

Day Seven

- Stabilize using Sulphite and Sorbate additions.

Day Ten

- Rack over 1 kg ripe bananas cut into small slices (no skins) and set aside for 2 weeks

Day Twenty-four

- Rack again, back sweeten to 9 Brix with remaining honey, and bulk age for 2 years before bottling

Trójniak 41
Created by: Marek Łęczycki

Winner: Second Place – Mazer Cup International 2013
Style: M4B Historical (Polish Trójniak)
Style: M2E Other/Mixed Fruit
Batch Yield: ~13 liters
ABV: Between 14-16%
Starting Brix: 14
Final Brix: 9

Ingredients

- Brewing Buckets, 15-liter (2 ea.)
- Strawberries: 2 kg
- Black Currant: 1 kg
- Gooseberries: 0.5 kg
- Raspberries: 620 grams (0.62 kg)
- Bilberries: 600 grams (0.6 kg)
- Banana: 1 fruit (without the skin) cut into small pieces
- Wildflower honey: about 4 liters (5.5 kg)
- Water: 5 liters
- Yeast, Lalvin 71B-1122: 10 grams
- Nutrient: Fermaid-O (or Activit-O)
- Nutrient: Diammonium Phosphate (DAP)
- Nutrient: GoFerm
- Pectic Enzyme (Powder): per manufacturer's direction
- Stabilizer: Sodium Metabisulphite
- Stabilizer: Potassium Sorbate

Yeast Starter

- Pour 250 ml of boiled water into a measuring cup
- Add 10 grams of sugar (Stir until completely dissolved)
- Allow starter to cool to 43C (109F) then add in 12.5 grams of GoFerm (Stir until completely dissolved)
- Allow additional time for starter to cool to about 38C (100F) then add the yeast.
- Slowly adjust temp down by adding a spoon of must every few minutes until starter temp is between 2-3C of your primary must before pitching

"LET THERE BE MELOMELS!" BY ROBERT RATLIFF

Directions:

Day One

- Before starting, clean and sanitize all of your equipment.
- Freeze all of the fruit you'll be using for this mead.
- Put all of the fruit into a 15-liter primary bucket and allow it to thaw.
- Thoroughly crush the fruit to release as much juice as possible.
- Add 1.5 liters of water.
- Blend in 0.5 kg of Wildflower honey.
- Check pH and adjust using Potassium Bicarbonate as directed under "CONTROLLING ACIDITY" until you reach a pH of ~3.4 (Stay above 3.2)
- When the temperature of the yeast starter and must are within a few degrees of tolerance, pitch the yeast and stir thoroughly to disperse it into the must.
- Add first dose of nutrients (Fermaid-O @ 0.4g/l by volume)
- Add Pectic Enzyme: per manufacturer's direction.
- Punch down the cap 2-3 times during the first 24 hours to maximize yeast contact, degas thoroughly, and to keep the fruits wet.

Day Three

- Remove the fruit and press as directed in "DEVELOPING YOUR PRIMARY" pouring the resultant juice into a 15-liter plastic brew bucket (w/airlock).
- Filter the remaining liquid through clean cheesecloth into the carboy as well to remove leftover fruit pieces and particulates. (Yield should be ~6 liters)
- Add 3.2 liters of water.
- Add enough Wildflower honey to reach Brix 26
- Add second dose of nutrients. (Fermaid-O @ 0.4g/l by volume)

Day Four

- Add the third and final dose of nutrients consisting of the following…
  - 0.4g/liter of Fermaid-O by volume
  - 0.6 g/liter of Diammonium Phosphate (DAP) by volume.

Day Seven

- Stabilize using Sulphite and Sorbate additions.

Day Twenty-one

- Rack and Backsweeten to Brix 9.
- Bulk age for 2 years before bottling

Trójniak 43
Created by: Marek Łęczycki

Winner: Second Place – Mazer Cup International 2014
Style: M4B Historical (Polish Trójniak)
Style: M2E Other/Mixed Fruit
Batch Yield: ~10 liters
ABV: Between 14-16%
Starting Brix: 17
Final Brix: 8

Ingredients

- Brewing Buckets, 15-liter (2 ea.)
- Josta berries: 1.1 kg (You can substitute 50/50 with gooseberries and black currants)
- Strawberries: 2.2 kg
- Banana: 200 g (ripe)
- Wildflower honey: 4 kg
- Water: 4.7 liters
- Potassium Carbonate (K2CO3): As needed
- Yeast, Lalvin 71B-1122: 10 grams
- Nutrient: Fermaid-O (or Activit-O)
- Nutrient: Diammonium Phosphate (DAP)
- Nutrient: GoFerm
- Pectic Enzyme (Powder): per manufacturer's direction
- Stabilizer: Sodium Metabisulphite
- Stabilizer: Potassium Sorbate

Yeast Starter

- Pour 250 ml of boiled water into a measuring cup
- Add 10 grams of sugar (Stir until completely dissolved)
- Allow starter to cool to 43C (109F) then add in 12.5 grams of GoFerm (Stir until completely dissolved)
- Allow additional time for starter to cool to about 38C (100F) then add the yeast.
- Slowly adjust temp down by adding a spoon of must every few minutes until starter temp is between 2-3C of your primary must before pitching

Directions:

Day One

- Before starting, clean and sanitize all of your equipment.
- Freeze all of the fruit you'll be using for this mead.
- Put the fruit into a 15-liter primary bucket and allow it to thaw.
- Thoroughly crush the fruit to release as much juice as possible.
- Add 1 liter of water.
- Blend in 500 g of wildflower honey.
- Check pH and adjust using Potassium Bicarbonate (K_2CO_3) as directed under "CONTROLLING ACIDITY" until you reach a pH of ~3.4 (Stay above 3.2)
- When the temperature of the yeast starter and must are within a few degrees of tolerance, pitch the yeast and stir thoroughly to disperse it into the must.
- Add first dose of nutrients (Fermaid-O @ 0.4g/l by volume)
- Add Pectic Enzyme: per manufacturer's direction.
- Punch down the cap 2-3 times during the first 24 hours to maximize yeast contact, degas thoroughly, and to keep the fruits wet.

Day Two

- Remove the fruit and press as directed in "DEVELOPING YOUR PRIMARY" pouring the resultant juice into a 15-liter plastic brew bucket (w/airlock).
- Filter the remaining liquid through clean cheesecloth into the carboy as well to remove leftover fruit pieces and particulates. (Yield should be ~4.2 liters)
- Add 3.7 liters of water.
- Add the balance of the wildflower honey. ~3.5 kg (to Brix 25)
- Check pH and adjust if necessary.
- Add second dose of nutrients. (Fermaid-O @ 0.4g/l by volume)

Day Three

- Add the third and final dose of nutrients consisting of the following…
  - 0.4g/liter of Fermaid-O by volume
  - 0.6 g/liter of Diammonium Phosphate (DAP) by volume.

Day Nine

- Add 200 grams of ripe banana cut into small pieces.

Day Fifteen

- Remove the banana and back sweeten to Brix 8.

Day Forty-five

- Sulphite & Sorbate to stabilize then rack and bulk age for 2 years before bottling.

Trójniak 54
Created by: Marek Łęczycki

Winner: Third Place – Mazer Cup International 2015
Style: M4B Historical (Polish Trójniak)
Style: M2E Other/Mixed Fruit
Batch Yield: ~5 liters
ABV: Between 14-16%
Starting Brix: 32
Final Brix: 8

Ingredients
- Brewing Buckets, 10-liter (1 ea.)
- Glass (or plastic) carboy, 10-liter (1 ea.)
- Hawthorn Berries: 2 kg
- Rose Hips: 0.5 kg
- Wildflower honey (1.7 liters or 2.4 kg)
- Water: 3.3 liters
- Yeast, Fermivin PDM: 10 grams
- Acid Blend: 2 grams/liter
- Nutrient: Fermaid-O (or Activit-O)
- Nutrient: Diammonium Phosphate (DAP)
- Nutrient: GoFerm
- Pectic Enzyme (Powder): per manufacturer's direction
- Stabilizer: Sodium Metabisulphite
- Stabilizer: Potassium Sorbate

Yeast Starter
- Pour 250 ml of boiled water into a measuring cup
- Add 10 grams of sugar (Stir until completely dissolved)
- Allow starter to cool to 43C (109F) then add in 12.5 grams of GoFerm (Stir until completely dissolved)
- Allow additional time for starter to cool to about 38C (100F) then add the yeast.
- Slowly adjust temp down by adding a spoon of must every few minutes until starter temp is between 2-3C of your primary must before pitching

Directions:
Day One

- Before starting, clean and sanitize all of your equipment.
- Use frozen fruits for this mead.
- Put all of the fruit into a 10-liter primary bucket.
- Allow fruit to thaw. Do not crush.
- Pour in all of the water then blend in enough honey to reach Brix 32.
- Check pH and adjust using Potassium Bicarbonate as directed under "CONTROLLING ACIDITY" until you reach a pH of ~3.4 (Stay above 3.2)
- When the temperature of the yeast starter and must are within a few degrees of tolerance, pitch the yeast and stir thoroughly to disperse it into the must.
- Add first dose of nutrients (Fermaid-O @ 0.4g/l by volume)
- Add Pectic Enzyme: per manufacturer's direction.
- Punch down the cap 2-3 times during the first 24 hours to maximize yeast contact, degas thoroughly, and to keep the fruits wet.

Day Two

- Add second dose of nutrients (Fermaid-O @ 0.4g/l by volume)
- Punch down the cap 2-3 times during the second 24 hours to maximize yeast contact, degas thoroughly, and to keep the fruits wet.

Day Three

- Add the third and final dose of nutrients consisting of the following...
  - 0.4g/liter of Fermaid-O by volume
  - 0.6 g/liter of Diammonium Phosphate (DAP) by volume.
- Punch down the cap 2-3 times during the second 24 hours to maximize yeast contact, degas thoroughly, and to keep the fruits wet.

Day Ten

- Remove the fruit and gently press (with your hands) to release the juice back into the must.
- Filter the must into a clean glass (or plastic) carboy using a clean cheesecloth to remove leftover fruit pieces and particulates.
- After 1- 2 weeks, or when Brix = 5, stabilize using Sulphite and Sorbate additions.
- Back sweeten with more honey to 8 Brix if needed.
- Add acid blend (2 grams/liter) to taste
- Set aside for 3-4 months to settle and clear.
- Rack once then bulk age for 2 years before bottling.

Trójniak 64
Created by: Marek Łęczycki

Winner: Third Place – Mead Free or Die 2015
Style: M4B Historical (Polish Trójniak)
Style: M2E Other/Mixed Fruit
Batch Yield: ~10 liters
ABV: Between 14-16%
Starting Brix: 22
Final Brix: 8

Ingredients

- Brewing Buckets, 15-liter (1 ea.)
- Glass (or plastic) carboy, 10 liter (1 ea.)
- Water: 2.7 liters
- Sour Cherries (w/pits): 2 kg
- Bird Cherries: 0.35 kg
- Bilberries: 0.6 kg
- Strawberry: 1 kg
- Black Currant: 0.5 kg
- Raspberry: 0.6 kg
- Wildflower honey: 4.2 kg
- Yeast, Enovini WS wine yeast: 10 grams
- Nutrient: Fermaid-O (or Activit-O)
- Nutrient: Diammonium Phosphate (DAP)
- Nutrient: GoFerm
- Pectic Enzyme (Powder): per manufacturer's direction
- Stabilizer: Sodium Metabisulphite
- Stabilizer: Potassium Sorbate
- Potassium Carbonate (K2CO3): As needed

Yeast Starter

- Pour 250 ml of boiled water into a measuring cup
- Add 10 grams of sugar (Stir until completely dissolved)
- Allow starter to cool to 43C (109F) then add in 12.5 grams of GoFerm (Stir until completely dissolved)
- Allow additional time for starter to cool to about 38C (100F) then add the yeast.

- Slowly adjust temp down by adding a spoon of must every few minutes until starter temp is between 2-3C of your primary must before pitching

Directions:

Day One

- Before starting, clean and sanitize all of your equipment.
- Freeze all of the fruit you'll be using for this mead.
- Put all of the fruit into a 15-liter primary bucket and allow it to thaw.
- Thoroughly crush the fruit to release as much juice as possible.
- Add 500 grams of honey (0.5 kg) and mix thoroughly.
- Add more honey (or a small amount of water) if needed to reach 21 Brix
- Check pH and adjust using Potassium Bicarbonate as directed under "CONTROLLING ACIDITY" until you reach a pH of ~3.4 (Stay above 3.2)
- When the temperature of the yeast starter and must are within a few degrees of tolerance, pitch the yeast into the primary bucket and stir thoroughly to disperse it into the must.
- Add first dose of nutrients (Fermaid-O @ 0.4g/l by volume)
- Add Pectic Enzyme: per manufacturer's direction.
- Punch down the cap 2-3 times during the first 24 hours to maximize yeast contact, degas thoroughly, and to keep the fruits wet.

Day Two

- Add second dose of nutrients (Fermaid-O @ 0.4g/l by volume)
- Punch down the cap 2-3 times during the second 24 hours to maximize yeast contact, degas thoroughly, and to keep the fruits wet.

Day Three

- Remove the fruit and press as directed in "DEVELOPING YOUR PRIMARY" pouring the resultant juice into a 10-liter glass (or plastic) carboy.
- Filter the remaining liquid into the carboy as well using a clean cheesecloth to remove leftover fruit pieces and particulates.
- Add the rest of the honey set aside for this batch (3.7 kg)
- Add the third and final dose of nutrients consisting of the following...
  - 0.4g/liter of Fermaid-O by volume
  - 0.6 g/liter of Diammonium Phosphate (DAP) by volume.
- Add ~2.7 liters of water to reach projected yield of 10 liters.

Day Twenty

- Stabilize using Sulphite and Sorbate additions.
- Back sweeten with more honey to 8 Brix.
- Set aside for 3-4 months to settle and clear.
- Rack once then bulk age for 2 years before bottling.

Trójniak 83
Created by: Marek Łęczycki

Winner: First Place – Valhalla 2016
Style: M4B Historical (Polish Trójniak)
Style: M2E Other/Mixed Fruit
Batch Yield: ~17 liters
ABV: Between 14-16%
Starting Brix: 16
Final Brix: 7

Ingredients

- Brewing Bucket, 20-liter (1 ea.)
- Glass (or plastic) carboy, 5 gallon (1 ea.)
- Sour Cherries (w/pits): 5.7 kg
- Strawberries: 2 kg
- Raspberries: 400 grams (0.4 kg)
- Wildflower honey (~7.2 kg)
- Water: 6.15 liters
- Yeast, Lalvin KIV-1116: 20 grams
- Nutrient: Fermaid-O (or Activit-O)
- Nutrient: Diammonium Phosphate (DAP)
- Nutrient: GoFerm
- Pectic Enzyme (Powder): per manufacturer's direction
- Stabilizer: Sodium Metabisulphite
- Stabilizer: Potassium Sorbate

Yeast Starter

- Pour 500 ml of boiled water into a measuring cup
- Add 20 grams of sugar (Stir until completely dissolved)
- Allow starter to cool to 43C (109F) then add in 25 grams of GoFerm (Stir until completely dissolved)
- Allow additional time for starter to cool to about 38C (100F) then add the yeast.
- Slowly adjust temp down by adding a spoon of must every few minutes until starter temp is between 2-3C of your primary must before pitching

Directions:

Day One

- Before starting, clean and sanitize all of your equipment.
- Freeze all of the fruit you'll be using for this mead.
- Put all of the fruit into a 20-liter primary bucket and allow to thaw.
- Pour in 1.15 liters of hot water and thoroughly crush the fruit to release as much juice as possible.
- Blend in ~700 grams (0.7 kg) of honey. (Enough to reach Brix 16)
- Check pH and adjust using Potassium Bicarbonate as directed under "CONTROLLING ACIDITY" until you reach a pH of ~3.4 (Stay above 3.2)
- When the temperature of the yeast starter and must are within a few degrees of tolerance, pitch the yeast and stir thoroughly to disperse it into the must.
- Add first dose of nutrients (Fermaid-O @ 0.4g/l by volume)
- Add Pectic Enzyme: per manufacturer's direction.
- Punch down the cap 2-3 times during the first 24 hours to maximize yeast contact, degas thoroughly, and to keep the fruits wet.

Day Three

- Remove the fruit and press as directed in "DEVELOPING YOUR PRIMARY" pouring the resultant juice into a 5-gallon glass (or plastic) carboy with airlock.
- Filter the remaining liquid through clean cheesecloth into the carboy as well to remove leftover fruit pieces and particulates. (Yield should be ~8.5 liters)
- Add 5 liters of water.
- Add the remaining honey to reach 27 Brix. (~ 6.0 kg)
- Add second dose of nutrients. (Fermaid-O @ 0.4g/l by volume)

Day Four

- Add the third and final dose of nutrients consisting of the following…
  - 0.4g/liter of Fermaid-O by volume
  - 0.6 g/liter of Diammonium Phosphate (DAP) by volume.

Day Fourteen

- Stabilize using Sulphite and Sorbate additions.
- Set aside for 3-4 months to settle and clear.
- Rack once then bulk age for 2 years before bottling.

Trójniak 102
Created by: Marek Łęczycki

Winner: Third Place – Mazer Cup International 2016
Style: M4B Historical (Polish Trójniak)
Style: M2C Berry
Batch Yield: ~10 liters
ABV: Between 14-16%
Starting Brix: 23
Final Brix: 7

Ingredients

- Brewing Bucket, 10-liter (1 ea.)
- Glass (or plastic) carboy, 3-gallon (1 ea.)
- Bilberries: 5 kg
- Wildflower honey: 4.3 kg
- Water: 3.5 liters
- Yeast, Lalvin EC-1118 Bayanus: 10 grams
- Nutrient: Fermaid-O (or Activit-O)
- Nutrient: Diammonium Phosphate (DAP)
- Nutrient: GoFerm
- Pectic Enzyme (Powder): per manufacturer's direction
- Stabilizer: Sodium Metabisulphite
- Stabilizer: Potassium Sorbate

Yeast Starter

- Pour 250 ml of boiled water into a measuring cup
- Add 20 grams of sugar (Stir until completely dissolved)
- Allow starter to cool to 43C (109F) then add in 12.5 grams of GoFerm (Stir until completely dissolved)
- Allow additional time for starter to cool to about 38C (100F) then add the yeast.
- Slowly adjust temp down by adding a spoon of must every few minutes until starter temp is between 2-3C of your primary must before pitching

Directions:
Day One

- Before starting, clean and sanitize all of your equipment.
- Freeze all of the fruit you'll be using for this mead.
- Put all the fruit into a 10-liter primary bucket and allow it to thaw.
- Thoroughly crush the fruit to release as much juice as possible.
- Pour in 0.5 liters of hot water and mix thoroughly.
- Blend in ~0.8 kg of Wildflower honey. (Enough to reach Brix 23)
- Check pH and adjust using Potassium Bicarbonate as directed under "CONTROLLING ACIDITY" until you reach a pH of ~3.4 (Stay above 3.2)
- When the temperature of the yeast starter and must are within a few degrees of tolerance, pitch the yeast and stir thoroughly to disperse it into the must.
- Add first dose of nutrients (Fermaid-O @ 0.4g/l by volume)
- Add Pectic Enzyme: per manufacturer's direction.
- Punch down the cap 2-3 times during the first 24 hours to maximize yeast contact, degas thoroughly, and to keep the fruits wet.

Day Three

- Remove the fruit and press as directed in "DEVELOPING YOUR PRIMARY" pouring the resultant juice into a 3-gallon glass (or plastic) carboy with airlock.
- Filter the remaining liquid through clean cheesecloth into the carboy as well to remove leftover fruit pieces and particulates. (Yield should be ~4.8 liters)
- Add 3 liters of water.
- Add the remaining 3.5 kg of Wildflower honey.
- Add second dose of nutrients. (Fermaid-O @ 0.4g/l by volume)

Day Four

- Add the third and final dose of nutrients consisting of the following…
  - 0.4g/liter of Fermaid-O by volume
  - 0.6 g/liter of Diammonium Phosphate (DAP) by volume.

Day Fourteen

- Stabilize using Sulphite and Sorbate additions.
- Back sweeten to Brix 8 and set aside for 3-4 months to settle and clear.
- Rack and bulk age for 2 years before bottling.

Trójniak 103 "Sofia"
Created by: Marek Łęczycki

Winner: Best of Show (Runner up) - Mazer Cup International 2016
Winner: Best of Show - Texas Mead Fest 2016
Style: M4B Historical (Polish Trójniak)
Style: M2E Other/Mixed Fruit
Batch Yield: 27 liters
ABV: Between 14-16%
Starting Brix: 22
Final Brix: 9

Ingredients
- Brewing Buckets, 33-liter (2 ea.)
- Sour Cherries (with pits): 9 kg
- Strawberries: 2 kg
- Blackcurrants: 1 kg
- Raspberries: 1 kg
- Bird Cherries: 0.5 kg
- Bilberries: 1 kg
- Water: 8 liters
- Wildflower honey: ~10.5 kg
- Yeast, Enovini WS wine yeast: 25 grams
- Nutrient: Fermaid-O
- Nutrient: Diammonium Phosphate (DAP)
- Nutrient: GoFerm
- Pectic Enzyme (Powder): per manufacturer's direction
- Stabilizer: Sodium Metabisulphite
- Stabilizer: Potassium Sorbate

Yeast Starter
- Pour 500 ml of boiled water into a measuring cup.
- Add 20 grams of sugar (Stir until completely dissolved)
- Allow starter to cool to 43C (109F) then add in 25 grams of GoFerm (Stir until completely dissolved)
- Allow additional time for starter to cool to about 38C (100F) then add the yeast.
- Slowly adjust temp down by adding a spoon of must every few minutes until starter temp is between 2-3C of your primary must before pitching

Directions:

- Before starting, clean and sanitize all of your equipment.
- Freeze all of the fruit you'll be using for this mead.
- Put all of the fruit into a 33-liter primary bucket and allow it to thaw.
- Manually crush the fruit while adding 2 liters of water to primary.
- Add 2 kg of Wildflower honey and blend thoroughly.
- Take a Brix reading then adjust using more water or honey to reach a Brix of 22.
- Check pH and adjust using Potassium Bicarbonate as directed under "CONTROLLING ACIDITY" until you reach a pH of 3.5
- When the temperature of the yeast starter and must are within tolerance, pitch the yeast into the primary bucket and stir thoroughly to disperse it into the must.
- Add first dose of nutrients (Fermaid-O@ 0.4g/l by volume)
- Add Pectic Enzyme: per manufacturer's direction.
- Punch down the cap 2-3 times daily and stir thoroughly to degas the must.
- After two (2) days, remove the fruit and press as directed in "DEVELOPING YOUR PRIMARY" pouring the resultant juice into the second 30-liter brewing bucket.
- Filter the remaining liquid through clean cheesecloth into the second brewing bucket to remove leftover fruit pieces and particulates.
- Add the remaining honey set aside (~ 8.5 kg) and 6 liters of water to reach the target yield.
- Check Brix and pH at this time. It should be roughly Brix 26 and a pH between 3.3-3.4 but as long as it remains above 3.2 you should be fine.
- Add second dose of nutrients (Fermaid-O @ 0.4g/l by volume)
- 24 hours later, add the third and final dose of nutrients consisting of the following...
  - 0.4g/liter of Fermaid-O by volume
  - 0.6 g/liter of Diammonium Phosphate (DAP) by volume.
- Final Brix should be ~9
- Stabilize with Sulphite and Sorbate then set aside for 3-4 months to settle and clear.
- Rack once then bulk age for 2 years before bottling.

Trójniak 104
Created by: Marek Łęczycki

Winner: Third Place – Mead Free or Die 2016
Style: M4B Historical (Polish Trójniak)
Style: M2E Other/Mixed Fruit
Batch Yield: ~25 liters
ABV: Between 14-16%
Starting Brix: 23
Final Brix: 7

Ingredients

- Brewing Buckets, 7-gallon (ea.)
- Glass (or plastic) carboy, 7 gallon (1 ea.)
- Black Currant: 2 kg
- Bilberries: 6.5 kg
- Sour Cherries (w/pits): 2.5 kg
- Strawberries: 2 kg
- Raspberries: 1.7 kg
- Wildflower honey: 11.6 kg
- Water: 5.8 liters
- Yeast, Enovini WS wine yeast: 20 grams
- Nutrient: Fermaid-O (or Activit-O)
- Nutrient: Diammonium Phosphate (DAP)
- Nutrient: GoFerm
- Pectic Enzyme (Powder): per manufacturer's direction
- Stabilizer: Sodium Metabisulphite
- Stabilizer: Potassium Sorbate
- Potassium Carbonate (K2CO3): As needed

Yeast Starter

- Pour 500 ml of boiled water into a measuring cup
- Add 20 grams of sugar (Stir until completely dissolved)
- Allow starter to cool to 43C (109F) then add in 25 grams of GoFerm (Stir until completely dissolved)
- Allow additional time for starter to cool to about 38C (100F) then add the yeast.
- Slowly adjust temp down by adding a spoon of must every few minutes until starter temp is between 2-3C of your primary must before pitching

Directions:

Day One

- Before starting, clean and sanitize all of your equipment.
- Freeze all of the fruit you'll be using for this mead.
- Put all the fruit into a 33-liter primary bucket and allow it to thaw.
- Thoroughly crush the fruit to release as much juice as possible.
- Pour in 1.3 liters of hot water and mix thoroughly.
- Blend in ~3 kg of Wildflower honey. (Enough to reach Brix 23)
- Check pH and adjust using Potassium Bicarbonate as directed under "CONTROLLING ACIDITY" until you reach a pH of ~3.4 (≥ 3.2)
- When the temperature of the yeast starter and must are within a few degrees of tolerance, pitch the yeast and stir thoroughly to disperse.
- Add first dose of nutrients (Fermaid-O @ 0.4g/l by volume)
- Add Pectic Enzyme: per manufacturer's direction.
- Punch down the cap 2-3 times during the first 24 hours to maximize yeast contact, degas thoroughly, and to keep the fruits wet.

Day Three

- Remove the fruit and press as directed in "DEVELOPING YOUR PRIMARY" pouring the resultant juice into a 6-gallon glass (or plastic) carboy with airlock.
- Filter the remaining liquid through clean cheesecloth into the carboy as well to remove leftover fruit pieces and particulates. (Yield should be ~15 liters)
- Add 4.5 liters of water.
- Add the remaining Wildflower honey to reach Brix 25 (~8.6 kg)
- Add second dose of nutrients. (Fermaid-O @ 0.4g/l by volume)

Day Four

- Add the third and final dose of nutrients consisting of the following…
  - 0.4g/liter of Fermaid-O by volume
  - 0.6 g/liter of Diammonium Phosphate (DAP) by volume.

Day Thirty

- Stabilize using Sulphite and Sorbate additions and set aside for 3-4 months.
- Back Sweeten to Brix 8 and bulk age for 2 years before bottling.

Trójniak 108
Created by: Marek Łęczycki

Winner: Third Place – Mazer Cup International 2017
Winner: Second Place – Mead Free or Die 2017
Style: M4B Historical (Polish Trójniak)
Style: M2E Other/Mixed Fruit
Batch Yield: ~31 liters
ABV: Between 14-16%
Starting Brix: 20
Final Brix: 7.5

Ingredients

- Brewing Buckets, 33-liter (2 ea.)
- Sour Cherries (with pits): 12 kg
- Blackcurrants: 2 kg
- Water: 11 liters
- Buckwheat honey: 4.5 kg
- Wildflower honey: 8.5 kg
- Yeast, Fermivin PDM: 20 grams
- Nutrient: Fermaid-O (or Activit-O)
- Nutrient: Diammonium Phosphate (DAP)
- Nutrient: GoFerm
- Pectic Enzyme (Powder): per manufacturer's direction
- Stabilizer: Sodium Metabisuphite
- Stabilizer: Potassium Sorbate

Yeast Starter

- Pour 500 ml of boiled water into a measuring cup
- Add 20 grams of sugar (Stir until completely dissolved)
- Allow starter to cool to 43C (109F) then add in 25 grams of GoFerm (Stir until completely dissolved)
- Allow additional time for starter to cool to about 38C (100F) then add the yeast.
- Slowly adjust temp down by adding a spoon of must every few minutes until starter temp is between 2-3C of your primary must before pitching

"LET THERE BE MELOMELS!" BY ROBERT RATLIFF

Directions:

Day One

- Before starting, clean and sanitize all of your equipment.
- Freeze all of the fruit you'll be using for this mead.
- Put the frozen fruit into a 33-liter primary bucket and allow it to thaw.
- Thoroughly crush the fruit to release as much juice as possible.
- Blend in ~2 kg of Wildflower honey. (Enough to reach Brix 20)
- Check pH and adjust using Potassium Bicarbonate as directed under "CONTROLLING ACIDITY" until you reach a pH of ~3.4 (Stay above 3.2)
- When the temperature of the yeast starter and must are within a few degrees of tolerance, pitch the yeast and stir thoroughly.
- Add first dose of nutrients (Fermaid-O @ 0.4g/l by volume)
- Add Pectic Enzyme: per manufacturer's direction.
- Punch down the cap 2-3 times per day to maximize yeast contact, degas properly, and to keep the fruits wet.

Day Three

- Remove the fruit and press as directed in "DEVELOPING YOUR PRIMARY" pouring the resultant juice into a 33-liter plastic brew bucket (w/airlock).
- Filter the remaining liquid through clean cheesecloth into the carboy as well to remove leftover fruit pieces. (Yield should be ~13.5 liters)
- Add 11 liters of water.
- Add remaining Wildflower honey and Buckwheat honey.
- Add second dose of nutrients. (Fermaid-O @ 0.4g/l by volume)

Day Four

- Add the third and final dose of nutrients consisting of the following...
  - 0.4g/liter of Fermaid-O by volume
  - 0.6 g/liter of Diammonium Phosphate (DAP) by volume.

Day Twenty

- Stabilize using Sulphite and Sorbate additions and back sweeten to Brix 7.5
- Set aside for 3-4 months to settle and clear.
- Rack and bulk age for 2 years before bottling.

Trójniak 109
Created by: Marek Łęczycki

Style: M4B Historical (Polish Trójniak)
Style: M2E Other/Mixed Fruit
Batch Yield: ~13.5 liters
ABV: ~ 14-16%
Starting Brix: ~33
Final Brix: 8
pH: 4.05

Ingredients
- Brewing Buckets, 15-liter (2 ea.)
- Buckwheat honey: 2 kg
- Wildflower honey: 3 kg
- Water: 7.3 liters
- Dried Rosehips: 1.8 kg
- Yeast, Fermivin PDM: 10 grams
- Nutrient: Fermaid-O (or Activit-O)
- Nutrient: Diammonium Phosphate (DAP)
- Nutrient: GoFerm
- Pectic Enzyme (Powder): per manufacturer's direction
- Stabilizer: Sodium Metabisulphite
- Stabilizer: Potassium Sorbate

Yeast Starter
- Pour 250 ml of boiled water into a measuring cup
- Add 20 grams of sugar (Stir until completely dissolved)
- Allow starter to cool to 43C (109F) then add in 12.5 grams of GoFerm (Stir until completely dissolved)
- Allow additional time for starter to cool to about 38C (100F) then add the yeast.
- Slowly adjust temp down by adding a spoon of must every few minutes until starter temp is between 2-3C of your primary must before pitching

Directions:

Day One

- Before starting, clean and sanitize all of your equipment.
- Put the rosehips into a 15-liter primary bucket and lightly crush.
- Pour in 7.3 liters of water
- Add 2 kg Buckwheat honey.
- Add 3 kg Acacia honey (Enough to reach Brix 33)
- Check pH and adjust using Potassium Bicarbonate as directed under "CONTROLLING ACIDITY" until you reach a pH of ~3.4 (Stay above 3.2)
- When the temperature of the yeast starter and must are within a few degrees of tolerance, pitch the yeast starter and stir thoroughly to disperse it into the must.
- Add first dose of nutrients (Fermaid-O @ 0.4g/l by volume)
- Add Pectic Enzyme: per manufacturer's direction.
- Punch down the cap 2-3 times during the first 24 hours to maximize yeast contact, degas thoroughly, and to keep the fruits wet.

Day Two

- Add second dose of nutrients. (Fermaid-O @ 0.4g/l by volume)

Day Three

- Add the third and final dose of nutrients consisting of the following…
  - 0.4g/liter of Fermaid-O by volume
  - 0.6 g/liter of Diammonium Phosphate (DAP) by volume.

Day Thirty

- Remove the fruit and lightly press the fruit pouring the resultant juice into a 15-liter plastic brew bucket (w/airlock).

Day Twenty-four

- Back sweeten to Brix 8.
- Stabilize using Sulphite and Sorbate additions.
- Rack mead, then bulk age for at least 3 years before bottling. (Rosehips take along time to age properly)

Trójniak 114
Created by: Marek Łęczycki

Winner: Gold Medal – Domras Cup 2017
Style: M4B Historical (Polish Trójniak)
Style: M2E Other/Mixed Fruit
Batch Yield: 15 liters
ABV: Between 14-16%
Starting Brix: 22
Final Brix: 8

Ingredients
- Brewing Buckets, 20-liter (2 ea.)
- Sour Cherries (with pits): 6 kg
- Strawberries: 1 kg
- Blackcurrants: 1 kg
- Water, room temperature: 3.5 liters
- Wildflower honey: ~5.6 kg
- Yeast, Fermivin PDM: 15 grams
- Nutrient: Fermaid-O (or Activit-O)
- Nutrient: Diammonium Phosphate (DAP)
- Nutrient: GoFerm
- Pectic Enzyme (Powder): per manufacturer's direction
- Stabilizer: Sodium Metabisulphite
- Stabilizer: Potassium Sorbate

Yeast Starter
- Pour 375 ml of boiled water into a measuring cup
- Add 15 grams of sugar (Stir until completely dissolved)
- Allow starter to cool to 43C (109F) then add in 18.75 grams of GoFerm (Stir until completely dissolved)
- Allow additional time for starter to cool to about 38C (100F) then add the yeast.
- Slowly adjust temp down by adding a spoon of must every few minutes until starter temp is between 2-3C of your primary must before pitching

Directions:
- Before starting, clean and sanitize all of your equipment.
- Freeze all of the fruit you'll be using for this mead.
- Put all of the fruit into a 20-liter primary bucket and allow it to thaw.
- Manually crush the fruit while adding 1 liters of hot water adjusting temperature of water to allow primary must to reach a temperature of around 30-32C.
- Add 1.2 kg of Wildflower honey and blend thoroughly.
- Take a Brix reading then adjust using more water or honey to reach a Brix of 21. (~1 liter)
- Check pH and adjust using Potassium Bicarbonate as directed under "CONTROLLING ACIDITY" until you reach a pH of ~3.4
- When the temperature of the yeast starter and must are within tolerance, pitch the yeast into the primary bucket and stir thoroughly to disperse it into the must.
- Add first dose of nutrients (Fermaid-O @ 0.4g/l by volume)
- Add Pectic Enzyme: per manufacturer's direction.
- Punch down the cap 2-3 times daily and stir thoroughly to degas the must.
- After three (3) days, remove the fruit and press as directed in "DEVELOPING YOUR PRIMARY" pouring the resultant juice into the second 20-liter brewing bucket.
- Filter the remaining liquid through clean cheesecloth into the second brewing bucket to remove leftover fruit pieces and particulates.
- Add the remaining honey set aside (~ 4 kg) and enough water (~2.5 liters) to reach the target yield.
- Check Brix and pH at this time. It should be roughly Brix 26 and a pH between 3.3-3.4 but as long as it remains above 3.2 you should be fine.
- Add second dose of nutrients (Fermaid-O @ 0.4g/l by volume)
- 24 hours later, add the third and final dose of nutrients consisting of the following…
  - 0.4g/liter of Fermaid-O by volume
  - 0.6 g/liter of Diammonium Phosphate (DAP) by volume.
- After about 2 weeks, or when Brix = 3.5, stabilize using Sulphite and Sorbate additions.
- Back sweeten with more honey to 8 Brix.
- Set aside for 3-4 months to settle and clear.
- Rack once then bulk age for 2 years before bottling.

Trójniak 117
Created by: Marek Łęczycki

Style: M4B Historical (Polish Trójniak)
Style: M2E Other/Mixed Fruit
Batch Yield: ~18 liters
ABV: Between 14-16%
Starting Brix: ~20
Final Brix: 8

Ingredients
- Brewing Bucket, 20-liter (1 ea.)
- Bilberries: 5.1 kg
- Sour Cherries (with pits): 1 kg
- Raspberries: 1 kg
- Black Currant: 1 kg
- Wildflower honey: 7.5 – 8.0 kg
- Water: 5.5 liters
- Yeast, Fermivin PDM: 20 grams
- Nutrient: Fermaid-O (or Activit-O)
- Nutrient: Diammonium Phosphate (DAP)
- Nutrient: GoFerm
- Pectic Enzyme (Powder): per manufacturer's direction
- Stabilizer: Sodium Metabisulphite
- Stabilizer: Potassium Sorbate
- Potassium Carbonate (K2CO3): As needed

Yeast Starter
- Pour 500 ml of boiled water into a measuring cup
- Add 20 grams of sugar (Stir until completely dissolved)
- Allow starter to cool to 43C (109F) then add in 25 grams of GoFerm (Stir until completely dissolved)
- Allow additional time for starter to cool to about 38C (100F) then add the yeast.
- Slowly adjust temp down by adding a spoon of must every few minutes until starter temp is between 2-3C of your primary must before pitching

Directions:

Day One

- Before starting, clean and sanitize all of your equipment.
- Freeze all of the fruit you'll be using for this mead.
- Put all of the fruit into a 20-liter primary bucket and allow it to thaw.
- Thoroughly crush the fruit to release as much juice as possible.
- Add 1 liter of water.
- Blend in 1 kg of Wildflower honey.
- Check pH and adjust using Potassium Bicarbonate (K2CO3) as directed under "CONTROLLING ACIDITY" until you reach a pH of ~3.4 (Stay above 3.2)
- When the temperature of the yeast starter and must are within a few degrees of tolerance, pitch the yeast and stir thoroughly to disperse it into the must.
- Add first dose of nutrients (Fermaid-O @ 0.4g/l by volume)
- Add Pectic Enzyme: per manufacturer's direction.
- Punch down the cap 2-3 times during the first 24 hours to maximize yeast contact, degas thoroughly, and to keep the fruits wet.

Day Three

- Remove the fruit and press as directed in "DEVELOPING YOUR PRIMARY" pouring the resultant juice into a 15-liter plastic brew bucket (w/airlock).
- Filter the remaining liquid through clean cheesecloth into the carboy as well to remove leftover fruit pieces and particulates. (Yield should be ~8.5 liters)
- Add 4.5 liters of water.
- Add ~5 kg of Wildflower honey to reach Brix 23.
- Add second dose of nutrients. (Fermaid-O @ 0.4g/l by volume)

Day Nine

- Add the third and final dose of nutrients consisting of the following…
  - 0.4g/liter of Fermaid-O by volume
  - 0.6 g/liter of Diammonium Phosphate (DAP) by volume.

Day Thirty

- Stabilize using Sulphite and Sorbate additions.

Day Sixty

- Rack then backsweeten to Brix 8 with more wildflower honey (~1.4 kg).
- Bulk age for 2 years before bottling.

Trójniak 121
Created by: Marek Łęczycki

Winner: Silver Medal – Mead Free or Die 2017
Style: M4B Historical (Polish Trójniak)
Style: M2D Stone Fruit
Batch Yield: ~10 liters   ABV: Between 14-16%
Starting Brix: 22 Final Brix: 8

Ingredients

- Brewing Buckets, 15-liter (2 ea.)
- Sour Cherries (very ripe w/pits): 8.5 kg
- Wildflower honey: 4.2 kg
- Yeast, Lalvin 71B: 10 grams
- Nutrient: Fermaid-O (or Activit-O)
- Nutrient: Diammonium Phosphate (DAP)
- Nutrient: GoFerm
- Pectic Enzyme (Powder): per manufacturer's direction
- Stabilizer: Sodium Metabisulphite
- Stabilizer: Potassium Sorbate
- Water only as directed for yeast starter.

Yeast Starter

- Pour 250 ml of boiled water into a measuring cup
- Add 10 grams of sugar (Stir until completely dissolved)
- Allow starter to cool to 43C (109F) then add in 12.5 grams of GoFerm (Stir until completely dissolved)
- Allow additional time for starter to cool to about 38C (100F) then add the yeast.
- Slowly adjust temp down by adding a spoon of must every few minutes until starter temp is between 2-3C of your primary must before pitching

Directions:

Day One

- Before starting, clean and sanitize all of your equipment.
- Freeze all of the fruit you'll be using for this mead.
- Put all of the fruit into a 15-liter primary bucket and allow it to thaw.
- Thoroughly crush the fruit to release as much juice as possible. This is very important since no additional water is used in this mead.
- Check pH and adjust using Potassium Bicarbonate as directed under "CONTROLLING ACIDITY" until you reach a pH of ~3.4
- When the temperature of the yeast starter and must are within a few degrees of tolerance, pitch the yeast into the primary bucket and stir thoroughly to disperse it into the must.
- Add first dose of nutrients (Fermaid-O @ 0.4g/l by volume)
- Add Pectic Enzyme: per manufacturer's direction.
- Punch down the cap 2-3 times during the first 24 hours to maximize yeast contact, degas thoroughly, and to keep the fruits wet.

Day Two

- Remove the fruit and press as directed in "DEVELOPING YOUR PRIMARY" pouring the resultant juice into the second 15-liter brewing bucket with airlock.
- Filter the remaining liquid through clean cheesecloth into the second brewing bucket to remove leftover fruit pieces and particulates.
- Add the honey to reach 30 Brix (4.2 kg)
- Add second dose of nutrients (Fermaid-O @ 0.4g/l by volume)

Day Three

- Add the third and final dose of nutrients consisting of the following…
  - 0.4g/liter of Fermaid-O by volume
  - 0.6 g/liter of Diammonium Phosphate (DAP) by volume.
- After about 2 weeks, or when Brix = 3.5, stabilize using Sulphite and Sorbate additions.
- Back sweeten with more honey to 8 Brix.
- Set aside for 3-4 months to settle and clear.
- Rack once then bulk age for 2 years before bottling.

Trójniak 134
Created by: Marek Łęczycki

Style: M4B Historical (Polish Trójniak)
Batch Yield: ~13.5 liters
ABV: Between 14-16%
Starting Brix: 32
Final Brix: 8

Ingredients

- Brewing Buckets, 15-liter (2 ea.)
- Dried Aronia Berries: 2.2 kg
- Hibiscus flowers (dried): 50 g
- Wildflower honey: 4.5 kg
- Water: 8 liters
- Yeast, Fermivin PDM: 10 grams
- Nutrient: Fermaid-O (or Activit-O)
- Nutrient: Diammonium Phosphate (DAP)
- Nutrient: GoFerm
- Pectic Enzyme (Powder): per manufacturer's direction
- Stabilizer: Sodium Metabisulphite
- Stabilizer: Potassium Sorbate

Yeast Starter

- Pour 250 ml of boiled water into a measuring cup
- Add 20 grams of sugar (Stir until completely dissolved)
- Allow starter to cool to 43C (109F) then add in 12.5 grams of GoFerm (Stir until completely dissolved)
- Allow additional time for starter to cool to about 38C (100F) then add the yeast.
- Slowly adjust temp down by adding a spoon of must every few minutes until starter temp is between 2-3C of your primary must before pitching

Directions:

Day One
- Before starting, clean and sanitize all of your equipment.
- Put the dried aronia berries into a 15-liter primary bucket.
- Add 8 liters of water.
- Blend in 4.5 kg of wildflower honey.
- Separately, add hibiscus flowers to 100 ml water and brew it into a tea.
    - Strain to remove the flowers, pour liquid into the must, then repeat this step with 100 more ml of water using same flowers.
    - Drain the second batch of liquid into the must and discard the flowers.
- Check pH and adjust using Potassium Bicarbonate as directed under "CONTROLLING ACIDITY" until you reach a pH of ~3.4 (Stay above 3.2)
- When the temperature of the yeast starter and must are within a few degrees of tolerance, pitch the yeast and stir thoroughly to disperse it into the must.
- Add first dose of nutrients (Fermaid-O @ 0.4g/l by volume)
- Add Pectic Enzyme: per manufacturer's direction.
- Punch down the cap 2-3 times during the first 24 hours to maximize yeast contact, degas thoroughly, and to keep the fruits wet.

Day Two
- Add second dose of nutrients. (Fermaid-O @ 0.4g/l by volume)

Day Three
- Add the third and final dose of nutrients consisting of the following...
    - 0.4g/liter of Fermaid-O by volume
    - 0.6 g/liter of Diammonium Phosphate (DAP) by volume.

Day Twenty
- Remove the fruit and lightly press the fruit pouring the resultant juice into a 15-liter plastic brew bucket (w/airlock).
- Back sweeten to Brix 8.
- Stabilize using Sulphite and Sorbate additions.

Day Sixty
- Rack and bulk age for two years before bottling.

AN ALTERNATIVE METHOD

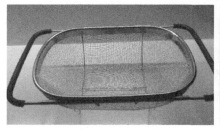 

In this section, we will approach the process a bit differently. The recipes listed in the previous section all used a starter with a specific process to develop it properly. The following recipes submitted by Mr. Jerzy Kaspersky do not use a starter. You'll also note that the duration the mead remains on the fruit varies quite a bit from the recipes submitted by Mr. Marek Leczycki in the previous section. Additionally, the fruit removal process is different. One method uses a fruit press while with the other uses a sieve or strainer. Both methods have their merits and as you can see, both methods produce award winning Polish Style meads.

What it comes down to is that there is more than one way to successfully make Polish meads. Learn both ways and when you're ready, adapt them to your own method and style. As long as the basics are adhered to you can call your final product Polish Style and mean it.

Trójniak Agrestniak
Created by: Jerzy Kasperski

Style: M4B Historical (Polish Trójniak)
Style: M2C Berry
Batch Yield: ~12 liters
ABV: Between 14-16%
Starting Brix: 36
Final Brix: 7

Ingredients

- Brewing Buckets, 20-liter (2 ea.)
- Gooseberries (frozen then thawed): 4.0 kg
- Water (Boiling): 6.6 liters
- Wildflower honey: ~4.6 kg
- Fermivin PDM wine yeast: 5 grams
- Nutrient: Fermaid-K (or Activit)
- Nutrient: Diammonium Phosphate (DAP)
- Pectic Enzyme (Powder): per manufacturer's direction
- Stabilizer: Sodium Metabisulphite
- Stabilizer: Potassium Sorbate

Yeast Starter

- Pour 100 ml of boiled water cooled to 38C into a measuring cup.
- Add yeast and let the mixture sit until yeast is fully rehydrated.
- Wait until the yeast is within 2-3 degrees of the must, then pitch.

Directions:

Day One

- Before starting, clean and sanitize all of your equipment.
- Freeze all of the fruit you'll be using for this mead.
- Pour 6.6 liters of boiled water into a 20-liter brewing bucket.
- Add 4 kg of honey and blend thoroughly.
- Take a Brix reading then add more honey (and/or water) until you have 10 liters total and have reached Brix 36.
- Put all of the fruit into a second 20-liter primary bucket and allow it to thaw.
- Thoroughly crush the fruit to release as much juice as possible.
- When the temperature of the yeast starter and must are within a few degrees of tolerance, pitch the yeast into the primary bucket and stir thoroughly to disperse it into the must.
- Add Fermaid-K @ 0.5g/l by volume: 5 grams
- Add Diammonium Phosphate (DAP) @ 0.5g/l by volume: 5 grams
- Add 1 dose of Pectic Enzyme: per manufacturer's direction.
- Punch down the cap 2-3 times daily during the first 3 days to maximize yeast contact, degas thoroughly, and to keep the fruits wet.

Day Fourteen

- Remove the fruit by filtering it through a sieve into a second 20-liter brewing bucket.
- Filter the remaining liquid through clean cheesecloth into the second brewing bucket to remove leftover fruit pieces and particulates.
- Pour into a glass carboy and add an airlock.

Day Twenty

- Final gravity should be ~Brix 7.
- Add Sulphite and Sorbate to stabilize.
- Set aside for 3-4 months to settle and clear.
- Rack once then bulk age for at least 4 years before bottling.

Trójniak Smorodyniak
Created by: Jerzy Kasperski

Style: M4B Historical (Polish Trójniak)
Style: M2C Berry
Batch Yield: ~10 liters
ABV: Between 14-16%
Starting Brix: 36
Final Brix: 7

Ingredients
- Brewing Buckets, 20-liter (2 ea.)
- Black Currants (fresh, destemmed, NOT crushed): 6.0 kg
- Water (Boiled): 6.6 liters
- Wildflower honey: ~4.6 kg
- Fermicru VR5 wine yeast: 5 grams
- Nutrient: Diammonium Phosphate (DAP)
- Pectic Enzyme (Powder): per manufacturer's direction
- Stabilizer: Sodium Metabisulphite
- Stabilizer: Potassium Sorbate

Yeast Starter
- Pour 100 ml of boiled water cooled to 38C into a measuring cup.
- Add yeast and let the mixture sit until yeast is fully rehydrated.
- Wait until the yeast is within 2-3 degrees of the must, then pitch.

Directions:

Day One

- Before starting, clean and sanitize all of your equipment.
- Pour 6.6 liters of boiling water into a 20-liter brewing bucket.
- Add 4 kg of honey and blend thoroughly.
- Take a Brix reading then add more honey (and/or water) until you have 10 liters total and have reached Brix 36.
- Rinse the Black Currants well then pour them into the must. Do NOT crush!
- When the temperature of the yeast starter and must are within a few degrees of tolerance, pitch the yeast into the primary bucket and stir thoroughly to disperse it into the must.
- Add Diammonium Phosphate (DAP) @ 0.8g/l by volume: 8 grams
- Add 1 dose of Pectic Enzyme: per manufacturer's direction.
- Punch down the cap 2-3 times daily during the first 5 days to maximize yeast contact, degas thoroughly, and to keep the fruits wet.

Day Fourteen

- Remove the fruit by filtering it through a sieve into a second 20-liter brewing bucket. Do not press the fruits.
- Filter the remaining liquid through clean cheesecloth into the second brewing bucket to remove leftover fruit pieces and particulates.
- Pour into a glass carboy and add an airlock.

Day Twenty-five

- Final gravity should be ~Brix 7.
- Add Sulphite and Sorbate to stabilize.
- Set aside for 3-4 months to settle and clear.
- Rack once then bulk age for 2 years before bottling.

Trójniak Wiśniak z Czeremchą

Created by: Jerzy Kasperski

Style: M4B Historical (Polish Trójniak)
Style: M2D Stone Fruit
Batch Yield: ~12 liters
ABV: Between 14-16%
Starting Brix: 36
Final Brix: 7

Winner: Gold Medal - M2D (Stone Fruit) – Mazer Cup International (MCI) 2016

Ingredients

- Brewing Buckets, 20-liter (2 ea.)
- Sour Cherries (very ripe w/pits): 4.0 kg
- Fresh Bird Cherries: 0.7 kg (Note: when picking the bird cherries, choose the least bitter fruit from the bushes available. If you feel the bitterness is too much, use less fruit)
- Water (Boiled): 6.6 liters
- Wildflower honey: ~4.6 kg
- Fermicru VR5 wine yeast: 5 grams
- Nutrient: Fermaid-K (or Activit)
- Nutrient: Diammonium Phosphate (DAP)
- Pectic Enzyme (Powder): per manufacturer's direction
- Stabilizer: Sodium Metabisulphite
- Stabilizer: Potassium Sorbate

Yeast Starter

- Pour 100 ml of boiled water cooled to 38C into a measuring cup.
- Add yeast and let the mixture sit until yeast is fully rehydrated.
- Wait until the yeast is within 2-3 degrees of the must, then pitch.

Directions:

Day One

- Before starting, clean and sanitize all of your equipment.
- Freeze all of the fruit you'll be using for this mead.
- Pour 6.6 liters of boiling water into a 20-liter brewing bucket.
- Add 4 kg of honey and blend thoroughly.
- Take a Brix reading then add more honey (and/or water) until you have 10 liters total and have reached Brix 36.
- Put all of the fruit into a second 20-liter primary bucket and allow it to thaw.
- Thoroughly crush the fruit to release as much juice as possible.
- When the temperature of the yeast starter and must are within a few degrees of tolerance, pitch the yeast into the primary bucket and stir thoroughly to disperse it into the must.
- Add Fermaid-K @ 0.5g/l by volume: 5 grams
- Add Diammonium Phosphate (DAP) @ 0.5g/l by volume: 5 grams
- Add 1 dose of Pectic Enzyme: per manufacturer's direction.
- Punch down the cap 2-3 times daily during the first 3 days to maximize yeast contact, degas thoroughly, and to keep the fruits wet.

Day Four

- Remove the fruit by filtering it through a sieve into a second 20-liter brewing bucket.
- Filter the remaining liquid through clean cheesecloth into the second brewing bucket to remove leftover fruit pieces and particulates.
- Pour into a glass carboy and add an airlock.

Day Twenty

- Final gravity should be ~Brix 7.
- Add Sulphite and Sorbate to stabilize.
- Set aside for 3-4 months to settle and clear.
- Rack once then bulk age for 2 years before bottling.

Trójniak Wiśniak

Created by: Jerzy Kasperski

Style: M4B Historical (Polish Trójniak)
Style: M2D Stone Fruit
Batch Yield: ~14 liters
ABV: Between 14-16%
Starting Brix: 36
Final Brix: 8

Winner: Silver Medal – Mead Free or Die (MFoD) 2017

Ingredients

- Brewing Buckets, 20-liter (2 ea.)
- Sour Cherries (very ripe w/pits): 6.0 kg
- Water (Boiled): 6.6 liters
- Rapeseed honey: ~4.6 kg
- Fermicru VR5 wine yeast: 5 grams
- Nutrient: Fermaid-K (or Activit)
- Nutrient: Diammonium Phosphate (DAP)
- Pectic Enzyme (Powder): per manufacturer's direction
- Stabilizer: Sodium Metabisulphite
- Stabilizer: Potassium Sorbate

Yeast Starter

- Pour 100 ml of boiled water cooled to 38C into a measuring cup.
- Add yeast and let the mixture sit until yeast is fully rehydrated.
- Wait until the yeast is within 2-3 degrees of the must, then pitch.

Directions:

Day One

- Before starting, clean and sanitize all of your equipment.
- Freeze all of the fruit you'll be using for this mead.
- Pour 6.6 liters of boiling water into a 20-liter brewing bucket.
- Add 4 kg of honey and blend thoroughly.
- Take a Brix reading then add more honey (and/or water) until you have 10 liters total and have reached Brix 36.
- Put all of the fruit into a second 20-liter primary bucket and allow it to thaw.
- Thoroughly crush the fruit to release as much juice as possible.
- When the temperature of the yeast starter and must are within a few degrees of tolerance, pitch the yeast into the primary bucket and stir thoroughly to disperse it into the must.
- Add Fermaid-K @ 0.5g/l by volume: 5 grams
- Add Diammonium Phosphate (DAP) @ 0.5g/l by volume: 5 grams
- Add 1 dose of Pectic Enzyme: per manufacturer's direction.
- Punch down the cap 2-3 times daily during the first 3 days to maximize yeast contact, degas thoroughly, and to keep the fruits wet.

Day Seven

- Remove the fruit by filtering it through a sieve into a second 20-liter brewing bucket.
- Filter the remaining liquid through clean cheesecloth into the second brewing bucket to remove leftover fruit pieces and particulates.
- Pour into a glass carboy and add an airlock.

Day Fifteen

- Final gravity should be ~Brix 8.
- Add Sulphite and Sorbate to stabilize.
- Set aside for 3-4 months to settle and clear.
- Rack once then bulk age for 2 years before bottling.

DWOJNIAK PREPARATION

Polish Dwojniak style meads are probably the most difficult you'll ever attempt. The specific gravity involved (Brix 45) will actually kill off most regularly used yeast strains. Margins for error are pretty slim and the costs involved could be prohibitive if you're not comfortable with attempting such high gravity meads. There's also the point that Dwojniak meads are designed to be aged for several years before drinking so time commitment is also a factor to consider before undertaking this type of project.

Only once you've reached an intermediate level in your brewing skills and are very comfortable with mead making processes should you attempt this complicated style of mead making.

This being said, if you're ready to try to make a Dwojniak, here's how you could go about it...

The first step is to develop a good starter as you normally would. It's at this initial point however that things immediately start to diverge from the standard process.

ENHANCING YOUR YEAST STARTER

Starting off with a good strong yeast strain is crucial, as most strains will not handle this mead no matter what you do. For the recipe provided we will be using Fermicru VR5. This particular strain of red wine yeast was developed to work well with difficult to ferment ingredients. It's also designed to help with color retention for recipes destined to be bulk aged for multiple years.

Anyway, the "toughening up" process takes about 48 hours so you might want to plan this batch to start on a Saturday morning and to progress over the course of the weekend finishing up on Sunday evening.

- First prepare about 1 liter of must.
  - 500 ml honey
  - 500 ml hot water
  - Adjust as necessary to Brix 45.
- Aerate it well and add 1g of DAP and Activit (or Fermaid)
- Set this aside for now.
- In a separate container, rehydrate your yeast.
  - Fermicru VR5 red wine yeast (2 grams/liter): 20 grams
  - Boiled water: 200 ml
- During first 5 hours add 15 ml (~ 1 tablespoon) of must to the yeast every 30 minutes.
- After 5 hours, increase the additions to 50 ml (~4 tablespoons).
  - Repeat at the higher dosage 3 or 4 times to complete the first day.
- On the second day, you will inoculate it 4 times. Space each one out throughout the day to allow the yeast more time between doses to toughen up as much as possible.

If your starter is bubbling along happily at the end of the second day, it is ready to pitch.

We begin this process by only making a 1-liter batch of must because there's a fair chance your starter will die. This is a truly difficult mead to make properly. If you make the entire batch of must right off and your starter dies on you, you'd be looking at another 48 hours before you could have a viable starter. If at the end of the 2 days your starter is healthy and bubbling nicely, then you can whip up the balance of your batch and pitch in a nice tough yeast colony. This will greatly increase the odds of a good final product.

Dwójniak Aroniak

Created by: Jerzy Kasperski

Winner: Best of Show – Mead Free or Die 2016
Style: M4B Historical (Polish Dwójniak)
Style: M2C Berry
Batch Yield: ~12 liters
ABV: Between 14-16%
Starting Brix: 46
Final Brix: 14

Ingredients:

- Aronia Berries (frozen then thawed): 4 kg (Late harvest fruits are best)
- Wildflower Honey: 7 kg
- Water: 5 liters
- Fermicru VR5 wine yeast: 20 grams
- Pectic Enzyme (Powder): per manufacturer's direction (In Poland, a liquid is used)
- Stabilizer: Sodium Metabisuphite
- Stabilizer: Potassium Sorbate
- Nutrient: Fermaid-K (or Activit)

"LET THERE BE MELOMELS!" BY ROBERT RATLIFF

Directions:

Day 1

- Prepare 1-liter of must to Brix 45.
  - 500 ml boiled water (Cool to 50C or 122F)
  - 500 ml honey
  - Adjust as necessary
- Rehydrate Fermicru VR5 yeast
  - 20 grams yeast
  - 200 ml boiled water (Cool to 50C or 122F)
- Start the toughening process
  - Add 15 ml of must every 30 minutes for 5 hours
  - After 5 hours, add 50 ml of must. This should be repeated a total of 3 or 4 times throughout the remainder of the day.

Day 2

- Add 100 ml of must. This should be repeated a total of 4 times throughout the day.
- If the starter is active and bubbling well after the final inoculation, you can proceed to creating the main batch of must. If not, then you'll need to start over with new yeast and a new 1-liter batch of must. (See above)
- In a clean 20-liter Brewing Bucket, blend 9 liters of must to Brix 46.
  - To create this accurately, first blend 4.5 liters of boiling water with 5.5 kg of honey.
  - Take a Brix reading
  - Add additional water honey to reach 46 Brix and 9 liters total volume.
- Place 4 kilos of aronia berries into a second 20-liter primary bucket and allow them to thaw.
- Thoroughly crush the fruit to release as much juice as possible.
- Add the crushed fruit and juice to the must and stir until fully incorporated.
- Add Pectic enzymes per manufacturer's instructions.
- Add Activit (or Fermaid-K): 10 grams
- Add DAP: 10 grams
- Pitch the yeast starter and mix thoroughly.

Days 3 through 7

- Punch the cap and aerate thoroughly twice daily.

Day 28

- Pour the must into a second 20-liter brewing bucket straining the fruit from it by pouring it through a sieve.
- Leave strained batch in a cool place to finish fermentation.

Day 60

- Sulphite and Sorbate to stabilize.

Day 90

- Rack and bulk age for 4-5 years.

GLOSSARY OF TERMS

Airlock – An Airlock or Fermentation Lock is a device used in beer brewing and wine making that allows carbon dioxide released during fermentation to escape the fermenter, while not allowing air to enter the fermenter, thus avoiding oxidation.

ABV (Alcohol by Volume) - is a standard measure of how much alcohol (ethanol) is contained (or potentially contained) in a given volume of an alcoholic beverage.

Auto-siphon - An auto-siphon is a simple piece of equipment that consists of a racking cane with tubing on one end, while the other end is housed within a racking tube. The racking tube will typically have a filter of some kind to block out unwanted particles and the racking cane will have a rubber grommet that allows easy movement within the tube while not allowing the passage of air.

Brix - Degrees Brix (symbol °Bx) is the sugar content of an aqueous solution. One degree Brix is 1 gram of sucrose in 100 grams of solution and represents the strength of the solution as percentage by mass.

Carboy – a carboy or demijohn is a glass or plastic vessel used in fermenting beverages such as wine, mead, cider, perry, and beer. Usually it is fitted with a rubber stopper and a fermentation lock to prevent bacteria and oxygen from entering during the fermentation process.

Cyser: A blend of honey and apple juice fermented together.

FG (Final Gravity) - The final targeted ratio of the density of a substance to the density of a reference substance; equivalently, it is the ratio of the mass of a substance to the mass of a reference substance for the same given volume.

Hydrometer – an instrument for measuring the density, or specific gravity of liquids.

Mead: An alcoholic drink made from honey, water, and yeast.

Melomel: A melomel is made using honey and any type of fruit addition. Depending on the fruit base used, certain melomels may also be known by more specific names (see cyser, pyment, and morat for examples). Possibly from the Greek *melomeli*, literally "apple-honey" or "treefruit-honey" (see also *melimelon*).

Must - This term is also used by mead makers for the unfermented honey-water mixture that becomes mead. Beer brewers would call this the wort.

OG (Original Gravity) - The initial targeted ratio of the density of a substance to the density of a reference substance; equivalently, it is the ratio of the mass of a substance to the mass of a reference substance for the same given volume.

Pyment: Pyment blends honey and red or white grapes. Pyment made with white grape juice is sometimes called "white mead".

Racking Cane - A racking cane is a hard plastic, glass, or stainless steel L shaped tube that eases the racking, or transferring, of your mead from one container to another with the assistance of a siphon tube. Racking canes often have a plastic piece on the end that allow the siphons suction to pull beer from just above the layer of dead yeast and sediment that could cause cloudiness in the final product.

Refractometer – A refractometer is an instrument for measuring a refractive index of a solution. In home brewing, a refractometer is used to measure the specific gravity before fermentation to determine the amount of fermentable sugars that will potentially be converted to alcohol.

Saccharomyces Bayanus - Is yeast of the genus Saccharomyces, and is used in winemaking and cider fermentation, and to make distilled beverages. Saccharomyces Bayanus like Saccharomyces Pastorianus is now accepted to be the result of multiple hybridization events between three pure species, Saccharomyces Uvarum, Saccharomyces Cerevisiae and Saccharomyces Eubayanus. Notably, most commercial yeast cultures sold as pure Saccharomyces Bayanus for wine making, e.g. Lalvin EC-1118 strain, have been found to contain S. Cerevisiae cultures instead. (Source: Wikipedia)

Saccharomyces Cerevisiae - Is a species of yeast. It has been instrumental to winemaking, baking, and brewing since ancient times. It is believed to have been originally isolated from the skin of grapes. (Source: Wikipedia)

SG (Specific gravity) is the ratio of the density of a substance to the density of a reference substance; equivalently, it is the ratio of the mass of a substance to the mass of a reference substance for the same given volume.

TOSNA – An acronym for Tailored Organic Staggered Nutrient Additions

BIBLIOGRAPHY

WEBSITES:

www.gotmead.com
Definitely one of the most comprehensive sources for mead and mead making currently available online. The owner (Ms. Vicky Rowe) has provided a plethora of great information and resources for beginning and experienced mead makers alike.

www.lallemandwine.com
The Lallemand website provides great information on wine making information and brewing statistics on their range of the yeast strains available from their company.

www.meadmaderight.com
Online calculators and some great information to assist you with your nutrient additions. The owner of Melovino Meadery (Mr. Sergio Moutela) has created a great source of information on the TOSNA 2.0 nutrient addition protocol as well as tips on proper yeast hydration and a recipe guide to assist you in creating a basic "traditional" mead successfully.

BOOKS:

Morse, Roger A., *"Making Mead (Honey Wine)"* Making Mead (Honey Wine). Wicwas Press, 1980

Ratliff, Robert, *"Big Book of Mead Recipes"*. GotMead Press, 2017

Schramm, Ken, *The Compleat Meadmaker*. Brewers Publications, 2003

Vargas, Patti & Gulling, Rich, *Making Wild Wines and Meads*. Storey Publishing, 1999

Zimmerman, Jereme, *"Make Mead Like A Viking"* Make Mead Like A Viking. Chelsea Green Publishing, 2015

INDEX

71B-1122, 20, 54, 58, 60, 64, 67, 84, 86, 88, 94, 98, 100, 127

ABV, 20, 21, 23, 32, 38, 40, 42, 44, 49, 54, 56, 58, 60, 62, 64, 67, 69, 72, 74, 76, 78, 80, 82, 84, 86, 88, 94, 96, 98, 100, 102, 104, 106, 108, 110, 112, 114, 116, 118, 121, 122, 123, 175

Airlock, 28, 175

Apple, 10, 14, 33, 35, 38, 40, 42, 44, 72, 74, 76, 78, 80, 82

Apricot, 14

Berry, 20, 27, 53

bilberries, 123

BJCP, 27, 182

Black Currant, 14, 33, 54, 84

black currants, 123

Blackberry, 14, 33, 34, 54, 56, 72, 84, 86, 88, 94, 96, 102

Blueberry, 14, 33, 34, 58, 74, 76, 84, 86, 88, 94, 96

Boysenberry, 15

Braggots, 8

Brix, 23, 25, 32, 38, 40, 42, 44, 49, 54, 56, 58, 60, 62, 64, 67, 69, 72, 74, 76, 78, 80, 82, 84, 86, 88, 94, 96, 98, 100, 102, 104, 106, 108, 110, 112, 114, 116, 118, 120, 122, 123, 124, 130, 132, 136, 138, 141, 143, 145, 147, 149, 151, 153, 155, 157, 159, 162, 164, 166, 168, 175

Cantaloupe, 15

Cherry, 15, 33, 34, 67, 82, 86, 94, 112

Coconut, 15, 34, 98, 106

Conversions, 31

Cranberry, 15, 33, 34, 56, 60, 62, 67, 74, 76, 78, 84, 88, 94, 96, 100, 102, 112

Cyser, 10, 33, 35, 38, 40, 42, 44, 72, 74, 76, 78, 80, 82, 145, 175

Cysers, 13, 20, 21, 27, 33, 35

Czwórniak, 121

D47, 20, 25, 69, 74, 106, 114, 116

DAP, 24

Dragon fruit, 15

Dwójniak, 121, 122, 123

Elderberry, 15, 34, 102

Fermaid, 24, 25, 26, 38, 39, 40, 42, 44, 49, 50, 54, 55, 56, 57, 58, 59, 60, 61, 62, 63, 64, 65, 67, 68, 69, 70, 72, 73, 74, 75, 76, 77, 78, 79, 80, 81, 82, 83, 84, 85, 86, 87, 88, 89, 94, 95, 96, 97, 98, 99, 100, 101, 102, 103, 104, 105, 106, 107, 108, 109, 110, 111, 112, 113, 114, 115, 116, 117, 118, 119

Fermax, 24

fermentation, 10, 23, 24, 25, 26, 61, 75, 79, 101, 121, 122, 123, 124, 125, 126, 127, 175, 176

Fruit, 1, 18, 20, 27, 66, 71, 123

GoFerm, 24, 38, 39, 40, 41, 42, 43, 44, 45, 49, 50, 54, 55, 56, 57, 58, 59, 60, 61, 62, 63, 64, 65, 67, 68, 69, 70, 72, 73, 74, 75, 76, 77, 78, 79, 80, 81, 82, 83, 84, 85, 86, 87, 88, 89, 94, 95, 96, 97, 98, 99, 100, 101, 102, 103, 104, 105, 106, 107, 108, 109, 110, 111, 112, 113, 114, 115, 116, 117, 118, 119, 127, 130, 132, 134, 136, 138, 141, 143, 145, 147, 149, 151, 153, 155, 157, 159

Gooseberry, 15

Grapes, 16, 49

Guava, 16

honey, 10, 13, 27, 35, 39, 41, 43, 45, 46, 50, 53, 55, 57, 59, 61, 63, 65, 68, 70, 73, 75, 77, 79, 81, 83, 85, 87, 89, 95, 97, 99, 101, 103, 105, 107, 109, 111, 113, 115, 117, 119, 120, 121, 122, 123, 124, 125, 175, 176, 182

Honeydew, 16

Hydrometer, 29, 30

K1V-1116, 20, 44, 49, 56, 62, 96, 102, 118

Kiwifruit, 16

Kumquat, 16

Lalvin, 20, 38, 40, 42, 44, 49, 54, 56, 58, 60, 62, 64, 67, 69, 72, 74, 76, 78, 80, 82, 84, 86, 88, 94, 96, 98, 100, 102, 104, 106, 108, 110, 112, 114, 116, 118, 127

Lemon, 16, 58

Lime, 16

Mandarin, 16

Mango, 16, 33, 34, 69, 104

Marionberry, 17

Mead, 8, 11, 12, 13, 15, 17, 20, 22, 23, 24, 25, 27, 33, 38, 39, 40, 41, 42, 43, 44, 45, 46, 49, 50, 53, 54, 55, 56, 57, 58, 59, 60, 61, 62, 63, 64, 65, 66, 67, 68, 69, 70, 71, 72, 73, 74, 75, 76, 77, 78, 79, 80, 81, 82, 83, 84, 85, 86, 87, 88, 89, 94, 95, 96, 97, 98, 99, 100, 101, 102, 103, 104, 105, 106, 107, 108, 109, 110, 111, 112, 113, 114, 115, 116, 117, 118, 119, 120, 121, 122, 123, 124, 125, 127, 129, 175, 176, 177, 182

Melomel, 13, 56, 58, 62, 64, 67, 69, 98, 108, 110, 114, 116, 118, 175

Melomels, 1, 8, 9, 13, 20, 27, 33, 66, 120

Metheglins, 8

Mulberry, 17

Must, 39, 41, 43, 45, 50, 55, 57, 59, 61, 63, 65, 68, 70, 73, 75, 77, 79, 81, 83, 85, 87, 89, 95, 97, 99, 101, 103, 105, 107, 109, 111, 113, 115, 117, 119, 175

Nectarine, 17

Nitrogen, 25, 32

Nutrients, 38, 40, 42, 44, 49, 54, 56, 58, 60, 62, 64, 67, 69, 72, 74, 76, 78, 80, 82, 84, 86, 88, 94, 96, 98, 100, 102, 104, 106, 108, 110, 112, 114, 116, 118

Orange, 17, 34, 69, 104, 106, 108, 110, 114, 116

Papaya, 17

Passionfruit, 17

Peaches, 17, 66

Pear, 18

Pectic Enzymes, 79, 95, 109, 124

Persimmon, 18

pH, 14, 15, 16, 17, 18, 19, 49, 126

Pineapple, 18, 34, 106, 108, 112, 114, 116

Plum, 18

Polish, 120, 121, 122, 123, 124, 127, 129

Pomegranate, 18

Primary, 38, 39, 40, 41, 42, 43, 44, 45, 49, 50, 54, 55, 56, 57, 58, 59, 60, 61, 62, 63, 64, 65, 67, 68, 69, 70, 72, 73, 74, 75, 76, 77, 78, 79, 80, 81, 82, 83, 84, 85, 86, 87, 88, 89, 94, 95, 96, 97, 98, 99, 100, 101, 102, 103, 104, 105, 106, 107, 108, 109, 110, 111, 112, 113, 114, 115, 116, 117, 118, 119, 124, 130, 132, 134, 136, 138, 141, 143, 145, 147, 149, 151, 153, 155, 157, 159, 162, 164, 166, 168

Pyment, 27, 33, 49, 176

Pyments, 13, 20, 27, 46

raspberries, 87, 95, 97, 101, 111, 123

Raspberry, 18, 33, 34, 62, 80, 86, 94, 96, 100, 110

RC-212, 20

Recipes, 8, 9, 10, 11, 12, 13, 28, 33, 120, 129, 177, 182

Red Currant, 18

Red Star, 20

Refractometer, 176

rosehips, 123

Secondary, 38, 39, 40, 41, 42, 43, 44, 45, 49, 50, 54, 55, 56, 57, 58, 59, 60, 61, 62, 63, 64, 65, 67, 68, 69, 70, 72, 73, 74, 75, 76, 77, 78, 79, 80, 81, 82, 83, 84, 85, 86, 87, 88, 89, 94, 95, 96, 97, 98, 99, 100, 101, 102, 103, 104, 105, 106, 107, 108, 109, 110, 111, 112, 113, 114, 115, 116, 117, 118, 119

sloes, 123

Specific gravity, 23, 176

Stone Fruit, 27

strawberries, 65, 119, 123

Strawberry, 18, 34, 64, 94, 96, 118

Sugar, 25, 32

Tamarind, 19

Tangerine, 16

TOSNA, 25, 26, 32, 176, 177

Traditionals, 20

Trójniak, 121, 122, 123, 127

Watermelon, 19

White Star, 20

Wyeast, 20
Yeast, 19, 24, 38, 39, 40, 41, 42, 43, 44, 45, 49, 50, 54, 55, 56, 57, 58, 59, 60, 61,
62, 63, 64, 65, 67, 68, 69, 70, 72, 73, 74, 75, 76, 77, 78, 79, 80, 81, 82, 83, 84,
85, 86, 87, 88, 89, 94, 95, 96, 97, 98, 99, 100, 101, 102, 103, 104, 105, 106,
107, 108, 109, 110, 111, 112, 113, 114, 115, 116, 117, 118, 119, 127, 130, 132,
134, 136, 138, 141, 143, 145, 147, 149, 151, 153, 155, 157, 159, 162, 164, 166,
168

ABOUT THE AUTHOR:

An experienced mead maker, Robert has been studying mead and its creative aspects since 2006. He has won multiple awards during competition with his meads at the Annual Mazer Cup International Mead Competition over the years and is regularly sought out for his input on recipe ideas. As a certified BJCP Mead Judge, Robert also enjoys offering pointers to entrants in upcoming competitions.

His extensive collection of meads, and mead recipes, has been gathered from around the world. A retired soldier (and former sailor), he is a veteran of the Kuwait, Iraq, and Afghanistan wars, has lived in 7 states, and visited most of the rest. Between his civilian and military careers, he has lived in or travelled to approximately 20 countries spanning the globe. Wherever he goes, he looks for local meads to sample and local mead makers with whom to share his knowledge with and to learn and unique local brewing techniques from.

When travelling, Robert tries to pick up a local varietal honey from each country he visits. His primary objective for this being to create a small batch of traditional mead from each country he visits. So far he has collected honey from 5 countries and hopes to add several more to the list before he retires and can finally start drinking them.

Mead making is not just an individual effort in the Ratliff family. His wife and two sons are also involved in the development of most of Robert's best recipes and he'll be the first to say that this will be a generational hobby in his household.

Robert, his family, and two cats currently live in Huntingdon, UK